# MATHS FORMULAE FOR SCHOOL STUDENTS

## – Clear your basic concepts

I0176298

**Sumita Bose**

V&S PUBLISHERS

*Published by*

**V&S PUBLISHERS**

F-2/16, Ansari Road, Daryaganj, New Delhi-110002
☎ 011-23240026, 011-23240027 • *Fax* 011-23240028
*Email* info@vspublishers.com • *Website* www.vspublishers.com

**Regional Office Hyderabad**
5-1-707/1, Brij Bhawan (Beside Central Bank of India Lane)
Bank Street, Koti, Hyderabad - 500 095
☎ 040-24737290
*E-mail* vspublishershyd@gmail.com

**Branch Office : Mumbai**
Jaywant Industrial Estate, 2nd Floor–222, Tardeo Road
Opposite Sobo Central Mall, Mumbai – 400 034
☎ 022-23510736
*E-mail:* vspublishersmum@gmail.com

Follow us on

All books available at **www.vspublishers.com**

© Copyright : V&S PUBLISHERS
**Edition 2017**

# Publisher's Note

After publishing various general trade and mass appeal books, V&S publishers, the fastest growing publisher of India, is pleased to bring out *'Maths Formulae For School Students'* the book which not only helps in understanding the basics of mathematical concepts but also provides the students with hints to arrive at the solution. To go through an examination successfully, the aspirants need to learn all the formulae and basics covered in the syllabus and increase their efficiency in solving the problems asked in the exams. While attending school and competitive examinations, students need to recollect and apply exact mathematical formulae. A candidate cannot reach the right solution until he/she makes use of the right formula. Therefore, application of the exact formula ensures the right solution and right answer to the question.

This book provides a quick glance at commonly needed formulae for Arithmetic, Algebra, Boolean Algebra, Geometry, Trigonometry, Coordinate Geometry, Dynamics and Statistics. The book is not only designed for the students and job aspirants but it is also a quick reference and handy guide for the teachers. This book contains relevant definitions to clear basic concepts, useful axioms, theorems and their properties, easy mnemonics for conversion of units, appendix containing mathematical constants, log tables and trigonometric tables. Many practical tips to boost the level of performance, attractive diagrammatic illustrations and usage of simple and lucid language make this book a unique piece of work.

We wish you success in all examinations and a very bright future in the field of mathematics.

Good Luck!!!

# Contents

# Introduction

Competitive examinations are mainly of two types – *entrance examination* (for admission purpose) and *recruitment examination* (for job purpose), whatever be the type, mathematics plays an important role. Like the crest of peacock, mathematics in the name of quantitative aptitude, quantitative ability, numerical ability etc. is at the head of all competitive examinations. This book is a resource help in navigating the labyrinth that is the preparation for competitive examination. The only method to score well in Mathematics is to clear the basic concept and memorize all the formulae followed by regular practice.

My sincere effort is to take away the uncertainty that crops up when a student knows the method of solving a problem but is not able to do so due to lack of remembrance of the associated formulae. This book is divided into different branches of Mathematics for easy navigation. It has comprehensive coverage of **Arithmetic, Algebra, Geometry, Trigonometry, Coordinate Geometry,** and **Statistics** Formulae. This book is not only designed for the students and job aspirants but it is also a quick reference and handy guide for the teachers.

# 15 Tips to Boost Your Performance

Every student aspires to get admission in a reputed college and every person taking a recruitment examination hopes to get his/her dream job. The following tips will help to go through the competitive examination and score high marks in them.

1. **Set your goal**

   The students should have a clear picture in their mind regarding their objectives and goals. They should make a choice and set their goals to become successful.

2. **Know about prerequisites**

   Prior to the preparation for any examination, the eligibility criteria should be determined. For example:

   (a) Age requirement for the examination

   (b) Required qualification

   (c) Required percentage of marks

3. **Ensure your planning is proper**

   Proper planning lays the foundation stone for any exam preparation. The first part of planning involves the knowledge of the following things:

   (a) Time of the year when the examination form is released

   (b) Number of times a particular examination is held in a year

   (c) Last date for submission of the form

   (d) List of things to be submitted along with the form, for example photographs, mark sheet etc.

   (e) Mode of payment for the examination fee – cheque, draft, credit card etc.

   The second part of the planning involves the knowledge of the examination pattern (stay updated as the syllabus and the examination pattern might change)

   (a) Subjects involved

   (b) Syllabus of each subject

   (c) Time duration of the examination

(d) Number of questions to be attempted

(e) Marking scheme (Check whether negative marking is a part of the scheme)

The third part is the preparation plan. The student has to decide whether he/she wants to join a coaching centre, some online course, study with friends or just do self study.

4. **Utilize all available resources**

   The students must make use of all possible resources. This includes good books, free online material, study material of seniors etc.

5. **Carry out SWOT analysis**

   SWOT stands for

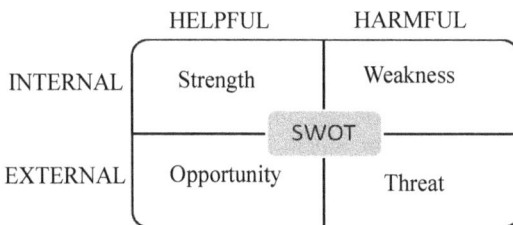

| | HELPFUL | HARMFUL |
|---|---|---|
| INTERNAL | Strength | Weakness |
| | SWOT | |
| EXTERNAL | Opportunity | Threat |

Identification of SWOT is important because it can help in improving the plan to achieve the objective. SWOT analysis can help the students to become more focused. Strength and weakness are internal factors whereas opportunity and threat are external factors.

*Strength*: The students need to identify their strength and enhance them to score well in the competitive examination.

*Weakness*: Identification of weakness will help the student to overcome it. The students should take professional help to do this if required.

*Opportunity*: The identification of opportunity will help the students to make the best use of it. For example, the students may exchange books or study material with their friends if possible.

*Threat*: Identification of threat will help the student to overcome it. For example, if the surrounding environment is too noisy during the afternoon the student can rest in the afternoon and study at night.

6. **Maintain self discipline**

   The preparation should be started well in advance. The students should not get easily diverted by the television shows, social media etc. Regularity is very important for the preparation.

7. **Clear basic concepts**

   This is especially important in Mathematics. Many students do not study Mathematics in Class XI, XII/College. As a result they tend to forget the basics. Hence, during preparation the chapters should be started right from the basics.

8. **Keep a positive attitude**

   Hellen Keller said, "Optimism is the faith that leads to achievement. Nothing can be done without hope and confidence." Hence, the students must work hard, remain confident and always keep a positive attitude.

9. **Optimize time management**

   Time management is about accuracy of choices.

   *Self Assessment*: The students can make a chart for self assessment. This will help in adjusting the time.

   *Weekly Schedule:* The best method of time management is to create a weekly schedule prioritizing the subjects/chapters. At the end of the week it should be evaluated. If the target is achieved, it can be ticked off otherwise the remaining portion can be noted down. The following chart can be made for weekly schedule:

| | *Mathematics* | | *English* | | *General Knowledge* | |
|---|---|---|---|---|---|---|
| | *Target* | *Done/ To do* | *Target* | *Done/ To do* | *Target* | *Done/ To do* |
| *Monday* | | | | | | |
| *Tuesday* | | | | | | |
| *Wednesday* | | | | | | |
| *Thursday* | | | | | | |
| *Friday* | | | | | | |
| *Saturday* | | | | | | |
| *Sunday* | | | | | | |

   *Peak Period:* Every person has his/her own peak period i.e. the time when they have maximum concentration. For example, some students may have their peak period during early morning others may have it late night. Difficult chapters should be done during this time.

| | |
|---|---|
| Class-School/College/Coaching | |
| Self Study | N |
| | U |
| | M |
| Transportation | B |
| | E |
| | R |
| Relaxation - TV, Net surfing etc. | O |
| | F |
| Physical Exercise | H |
| | O |
| | U |
| Daily routine (Brush, bath etc.) | R |
| | S |
| Sleep/Rest | |

*Self Reward* : Some self rewards like watching a movie or a favourite TV programme can be awarded if the weekly schedule is accomplished.

10. **Solve mock test**

    After completing the syllabus the students should solve the past year papers, the sample papers as well as the practice test papers. Many coaching institutes offer test series. The students may join them to gain more confidence.

11. **Do physical exercise**

    This is a must for every person throughout the year. Physical exercise keeps a person healthy and improves blood circulation, oxygenates the body, boosts decision making skills, improves memory, increases attention span etc.

12. **Minimise stress**

    It is natural to be tensed, stressed and anxious before any examination. Physical exercise is one of the best stress busters. Apart from physical exercise, one can practice 'Pranayam' (breathing exercise) and meditation to reduce stress.

13. **Eat a balanced diet**

    A balanced diet is very important to keep the body as well as the brain healthy. The students should stop eating any junk food about two months prior to the examination. Some of the foods which increase brain power are whole grains, lentil, pomegranate juice, nuts, avocado, little quantity of dark chocolate etc. All these food release memory-enhancing chemicals and help to focus.

14. **Drink adequate water**

Water enhances mental function. The brain may get dehydrated in the absence of adequate water. Hence, the students should drink at least 8-10 glasses of water everyday.

15. **Have a good night's sleep**

Along with proper diet and adequate water, 7-8 hours of sleep is very important to be successful. Good sleep improves concentration, memory and grades. It lowers stress and anxiety.

# (1) Arithmetic Formulae

## Types of Numbers

a) **Natural Number**

Counting numbers starting from one are called natural numbers. It is represented by the symbol N. 1, 2, 3 ...

b) **Whole Number**

Natural numbers along with zero are called whole numbers. It is represented by the symbol W. 0, 1, 2, 3 ...

c) **Integer**

Natural numbers, zero along with negative numbers together form the integers. It is represented by the symbol Z.

... –3, –2, –1, 0, 1, 2, 3 ...

d) **Even Number**

A number which is divisible by two is called an even number.

2, 4, 6, 8 ...

e) **Odd Number**

A number which is not divisible by two is called an odd number.

1, 3, 5, 7 ...

f) **Prime Number**

A number which has only two factors one and itself is called a prime number. There are 25 prime numbers between 1 and 100. They are: 2, 3, 5, 7, 11, 13, 17, 19, 23, 29, 31, 37, 41, 43, 47, 53, 59, 61, 67, 71, 73, 79, 83, 89 and 97.

g) **Twin Prime**

A twin prime is a prime number that differs from another prime number by two. For example, 3 and 5, 5 and 7 ...

h) **Composite Number**

A number which has more than two factors is called a composite number. 4, 6, 8, 9, 10, 12, 14, 15, 16, 18 ...

i) **Co-prime Number**

Two numbers are said to be co-prime or relatively prime if their HCF is 1. For example, 2, 3 ; 3, 7 ...

**Properties of prime and co-prime numbers**

(i)   1 is neither prime nor composite.

(ii)  2 is the only even prime number.

(iii) Let $p$ be a prime number. If $p$ divides $a^2$, then $p$ divides $a$, where $a$ is a positive integer.

(iv)  All prime numbers are co-prime to each other.

(v)   Any two consecutive integers are always co-prime.

(vi)  Sum of any two co-prime numbers is always co-prime with their product.

(vii) 1 is co-prime with all numbers.

**Fundamental Theorem of Arithmetic:** Every composite number can be factorized as a product of primes. This factorization is unique apart from the order in which prime factors occur.

j)   **Rational Number**

A number which can be put in the form p/q where $p$ and $q$ are integers and $q \neq 0$ is called a rational number. It is represented by the symbol Q. For example, –3/5, 19, 2/9...

**Properties of rational number**

(i)   There are infinitely many rational numbers between any two given rational numbers.

(ii)  If $x = p/q$ be a rational number, such that the prime factorisation of $q$ is of the form $2^n5^m$, where $n, m$ are non-negative integers, then $x$ has a decimal expansion which terminates.

(iii) If $x = p/q$ be a rational number, such that the prime factorisation of $q$ is not of the form $2^n5^m$, where $n, m$ are non-negative integers, then $x$ has a decimal expansion which is non-terminating repeating.

(iv)  Rational numbers are either terminating or non-terminating recurring decimal.

k)   **Irrational Number**

A number which is neither terminating nor non-terminating repeating is known as an irrational number. For example, $\sqrt{2}$, $\sqrt{3}$, $\sqrt{5}$ ...

l)   **Real Number**

Rational numbers along with irrational numbers are known as real numbers. For example, 7/8, 23, $\sqrt{7}$ ... Every real number can be uniquely represented on a number line.

**Note:** If $r$ is a rational number other than 0 and $s$ is an irrational number, then $r + s$, $r - s$, $r \times s$ and $r \div s$ are irrational numbers.

**Properties of real numbers**

For any real numbers a, b and c,

(i)   **Closure Property of Addition**
      Sum (or difference) of two real numbers equals a real number.

(ii)  **Additive Identity**
      $a + 0 = a$

(iii) **Additive Inverse**
      $a + (-a) = 0$

(iv)  **Associative Property of Addition**
      $(a + b) + c = a + (b + c)$

(v)   **Commutative Property of Addition**
      $a + b = b + a$

(vi)  **Definition of Subtraction**
      $a - b = a + (-b)$

(vii) **Closure Property of Multiplication**
      Product (or quotient if denominator $\neq 0$) of two real numbers equals a real number

(viii) **Multiplicative Identity**
      $a \times 1 = a$

(ix)  **Multiplicative Inverse**
      $a \times (1/a) = 1 \ (a \neq 0)$

(x)   **Multiplication by zero**
      $a \times 0 = 0$

(xi)  **Commutative Property of Multiplication**
      $a \times b = b \times a$

(xii) **Associative Property of Multiplication**
      $(a \times b) \times c = a \times (b \times c)$

(xiii) **Distributive Law**
      $a(b + c) = ab + ac$

(xiv) **Definition of Division**
      $$\frac{a}{b} = a\left(\frac{1}{b}\right)$$

# Even-Odd Relations

- Odd Integer × Odd Integer = Odd Integer
- Even Integer × Even Integer = Even Integer
- Odd Integer × Even Integer = Even Integer
- Odd Integer + Odd Integer = Even Integer
- Odd Integer − Odd Integer = Even Integer

- Even Integer + Even Integer = Even Integer
- Even Integer – Even Integer = Even Integer
- $(Odd)^{Odd} = Odd$
- $(Even)^{Even} = Even$
- $(Even)^{Odd} = Even$

## Rules for Integer Operations

### Addition (When signs are the same)
(i) Keep the sign.
(ii) Add.

### Addition (When signs are different)
1. Keep the sign of the number that is farthest from zero.
2. Subtract the smaller number from the bigger number.

### Subtraction
1. Change the subtraction sign to an addition sign.
2. Change the sign of the second number.
3. Follow addition rules.

### Multiplication/Division
1. If there is an even number of negative signs, the answer will be positive.
2. If there is an odd number of negative signs, the answer will be negative.

## ═══════BINARY NUMBER SYSTEM═══════

### Decimal Number System
The number system which uses ten digits- 0, 1, 2, 3, 4, 5, 6, 7, 8 and 9 is known as decimal number system.

### Binary Number System
The number system which uses only two digits 0 and 1 is known as binary number system.

*Note*: Computers use binary digits commonly known as bit.

In computers,

1 Byte = 8 bits
1 Kilobyte = 1024 Byte
1 Megabyte = 1024 Kilobyte
1 Gigabyte = 1024 Megabyte
1 Terabyte = 1024 Gigabyte

Maths Formulae For School Students

## Base of a Number System

The base of a number system is equal to the number of digits used in that system.

- The base of decimal system is 10.
- The base of binary system is 2.

## Decimal to Binary Conversion

(i) Divide the number of the decimal system by 2.

(ii) Write the remainder as 0 if there is no remainder.

(iii) Divide the quotient by 2.

(iv) Continue the process till the quotient becomes 0 and the remainder is 1.

(v) Write the remainder from down upwards in left to right manner to get the binary number.

## Binary to Decimal Conversion

1. Write the binary number.
2. Write $2^0$, $2^1$, $2^2$, $2^3$, $2^4$, ... under each digit of the binary number starting from the right.
3. Cross out those powers of 2 which are under 0 of the binary number.
4. Add the remaining powers of 2.

## Binary Addition

a) $0 + 0 = 0$

b) $0 + 1 = 1$

c) $1 + 0 = 1$

d) $1 + 1 = 0$ (carry 1)

## Binary Subtraction

a) $0 - 0 = 0$

b) $1 - 0 = 1$

c) $1 - 1 = 0$

d) $10 - 1 = 1$

e) $0 - 1 =$ Borrow 1

## Binary Multiplication

a) $0 \times 0 = 0$

b) $0 \times 1 = 0$

c) $1 \times 0 = 0$

d) $1 \times 1 = 1$

## Binary Division

Binary division is similar to decimal long division.

*Note:* All fractions do not have an exact binary representation.

## FACTORS AND MULTIPLES

**Factor :** A number is a factor of another number if the second number is divisible by the first number. For example, 2 is a factor of 8.

**Multiple :** A number is a multiple of another number if it is divisible by the second number. For example, 6 is a multiple of 3.

## Properties of Factors

    (i)  Every natural number is a factor of itself.

    (ii)  1 is the factor of every number.

    (iii) Every number is a factor of zero.

    (iv) Every number other than 1 has at least two factors, namely the number itself and 1.

## Properties of Multiples

    (i)  Every number is a multiple of 1.

    (ii)  Every number is a multiple of itself.

    (iii) Zero (0) is a multiple of every number.

    (iv) Every multiple except zero is either equal to or greater than any of its factors.

    (v)  The product of two or more factors is the multiple of each factor.

    (vi) There are infinite multiples of any number.

## Divisibility Rules

| Divisible by | Rule |
|---|---|
| 2 | The last digit is even 0, 2, 4, 6, 8 |
| 3 | The sum of the digits is divisible by 3 |
| 4 | The last 2 digits are divisible by 4 |
| 5 | The last digit is 0 or 5 |
| 6 | The number is divisible by both 2 and 3 |
| 7 | Double the last digit and subtract it from the rest of the number. If the answer is: 0, or divisible by 7 (The process may be repeated several times) |
| 8 | The last three digits are divisible by 8 |

Maths Formulae For School Students

| 9 | The sum of the digits is divisible by 9 |
| 10 | The number ends in 0 |
| 11 | If the difference between the sum of the digits at odd places and the sum of the digits at even places is 0, or divisible by 11 |
| 12 | The number is divisible by both 3 and 4 |

## Euclid's Division Lemma

Given positive integers $a$ and $b$, there exist unique integers $q$ and $r$ satisfying $a = bq + r$ where $0 \le r < b$.

*Note:* A *lemma* is a proven statement used for proving another statement.

## Euclid's Division Algorithm

The HCF of any two positive integers $c$ and $d$, with $c > d$, is obtained as follows:

1. Apply the division lemma to find $q$ and $r$ where $c = dq + r$ and $0 \le r < d$.
2. If $r = 0$, the HCF is $d$. If $r \ne 0$, apply Euclid's lemma to $d$ and $r$.
3. Continue the process till the remainder is zero. The divisor at this stage will be HCF $(c, d)$.
   Also, HCF$(c, d)$ = HCF$(d, r)$.

*Note:* An *algorithm* is a series of well defined steps which give a procedure for solving a type of problem.

## LCM and HCF

If $a$ and $b$ are positive integers then,

   LCM $(a, b)$ × HCF $(a, b) = a \times b$

   If $a, b, c$ are positive integers then,

   LCM $(a, b, c)$ × HCF $(a, b, c) \ne a \times b \times c$

   $$\text{LCM } (a, b, c) = \frac{a.b.c \, \text{HCF}(a,b,c)}{\text{HCF}(a,b).\text{HCF}(b,c).\text{HCF}(a,c)}$$

   $$\text{HCF } (a, b, c) = \frac{a.b.c \, \text{LCM}(a,b,c)}{\text{LCM}(a,b).\text{LCM}(b,c).\text{LCM}(a,c)}$$

## ═══════ FRACTION AND DECIMAL ═══════

## Types of Fractions

### Vulgar Fraction

A fraction consisting of an integer numerator and a non-zero denominator is called a common or a vulgar fraction.

For example, $\dfrac{9}{7}, \dfrac{3}{4}$

## Proper Fraction
Fractions whose numerators are less than the denominators are called proper fractions.

For example, $\dfrac{3}{7}, \dfrac{8}{11}$

## Improper Fraction
Fractions with the numerator either equal to or greater than the denominator are called improper fraction.

For example, $\dfrac{91}{23}, \dfrac{3}{2}$

## Mixed Fraction
A combination of a proper fraction and a whole number is called a mixed fraction. For example, 21/3, 42/5

## Properties of Fractions

(i)   Addition $\dfrac{a}{b} + \dfrac{c}{d} = \dfrac{ad + bc}{bd}$

(ii)  Subtraction $\dfrac{a}{b} - \dfrac{c}{d} = \dfrac{ad - bc}{bd}$

(iii) Multiplication $\dfrac{a}{b} \times \dfrac{c}{d} = \dfrac{ac}{bd}$

(iv)  Division $\dfrac{\frac{a}{b}}{\frac{c}{d}} = \dfrac{a}{b} \div \dfrac{c}{d} = \dfrac{a}{b} \times \dfrac{d}{c} = \dfrac{ad}{bc}$

(v)   The value of a fraction is not altered if both the numerator and denominator are multiplied or divided by the same number.

(vi)  Reciprocal of a is $\dfrac{1}{a}$ .

(vii) 1 and -1 are reciprocal of itself.

(viii) The reciprocal of zero does not exist.

## Properties of Decimals

(i)  A decimal fraction does not change if we add some zeros to the right of it. For example, 14.7 = 14.7000

(ii) A decimal fraction does not change if zeros are omitted from the end. For example, 0.00456000 = 0.00456

(iii)A decimal fraction will be increased by 10, 100, 1000,... times if the decimal point is shifted by one, two, three, ... places to the right respectively.

(iv) A decimal fraction will be decreased by 10, 100,1000,... times if the decimal point is shifted by one, two, three, ... places to the left respectively.

## ═══════ SQUARE AND SQUARE ROOT ═══════

If a natural number $m$ can be expressed as $n^2$ i.e. $m = n \times n$, where $n$ is also a natural number, then $m$ is a **square number**. Square numbers are also called perfect squares.

It is useful to memorize the square of first twenty natural numbers.

| Number | Square | Number | Square |
|--------|--------|--------|--------|
| 1 | 1 | 11 | 121 |
| 2 | 4 | 12 | 144 |
| 3 | 9 | 13 | 169 |
| 4 | 16 | 14 | 196 |
| 5 | 25 | 15 | 225 |
| 6 | 36 | 16 | 256 |
| 7 | 49 | 17 | 289 |
| 8 | 64 | 18 | 324 |
| 9 | 81 | 19 | 361 |
| 10 | 100 | 20 | 400 |

## Properties of Square Numbers

(i) All square numbers end with 0, 1, 4, 5, 6 or 9 at unit's place.

(ii) (a) If the last digit of a number is 1 or 9, its square ends in 1 and the number formed by its preceding digits must be divisible by four.

(b) If the last digit of a number is 2 or 8, its square ends in 4 and the preceding digit must be even.

(c) If the last digit of a number is 3 or 7, its square ends in 9 and the number formed by its preceding digits must be divisible by four.

(d) If the last digit of a number is 4 or 6, its square ends in 6 and the preceding digit must be odd.

(e) If the last digit of a number is 5, its square ends in 25.

(iii) A natural number having 2, 3, 7 or 8 at the one's place is never a perfect square.

(iv) A natural number with 0, 1, 4, 5, 6 or 9 at the one's place may or may not be a square number. Eg. 121 is a square number but 221 is not a square number.

(v) The square of an even natural number is always even.

(vi) The square of an odd natural number is always odd.

(vii) The square of any odd number can be expressed as the sum of two consecutive positive integers.

(viii) Square numbers can only have even number of zeros at the end.

(ix) Factors of every square number can be grouped in pairs.

(x) There are *2n* non perfect square numbers between any two consecutive square numbers *n* and *(n + 1)*.

(xi) A *n* digit natural number has either *2n* or *2n -1* digits in its square.

(xii) A perfect square leaves a remainder 0 or 1 when divided by 3.

(xiii) A perfect square can be expressed as a sum of successive odd natural numbers starting with 1.

(xiv) The square of any odd natural number can be expressed as the sum of two consecutive positive integers.

(xv) The square of a natural number greater than 1 can be written as
  (a) multiple of 3 or multiple of 3 plus 1.
  (b) multiple of 4 or multiple of 4 plus 1.

## Square Root

Square root is the inverse operation of square. In other words, square root of a number $a$ is a number $y$ such that $y^2 = a$.

## Properties of Square Root

(i) Every non-negative real number $a$ has a unique non-negative square root, called the principal square root, which is denoted by $\sqrt{a}$.

(ii) Every positive number $a$ has two square roots: $\sqrt{a}$, which is positive, and $-\sqrt{a}$, which is negative. Together, these two roots are denoted as $\pm\sqrt{a}$.

(iii) The square root of $x$ is rational if and only if $x$ is a rational number that can be represented as a ratio of two perfect squares.

$$\sqrt{x^2} = |x| = \begin{cases} x, & \text{if } x \geq 0 \\ -x, & \text{if } x < 0. \end{cases}$$

(iv) For all real numbers $x$

(v) $\sqrt{xy} = \sqrt{x}\sqrt{y}$ For all non-negative real numbers $x$ and $y$,

$$\sqrt{\frac{x}{y}} = \frac{\sqrt{x}}{\sqrt{y}} \text{ where } x > 0, y > 0$$

(vi) If a perfect square is of $n$ digits, then its square root has $\frac{n}{2}$ digits if $n$ is even and $\frac{(n+1)}{2}$ if $n$ is odd.

Numbers obtained when a number is multiplied by itself three times are known as cube numbers. In other words, a natural number $n$ is a perfect cube, if there exists a natural number $m$ such that:

$n = m \times m \times m = m^3$

It is useful to memorize the cube of first twenty natural numbers.

| Number | Cube | Number | Cube |
|--------|------|--------|------|
| 1 | 1 | 11 | 1331 |
| 2 | 8 | 12 | 1728 |
| 3 | 27 | 13 | 2197 |
| 4 | 64 | 14 | 2744 |
| 5 | 125 | 15 | 3375 |
| 6 | 216 | 16 | 4096 |
| 7 | 343 | 17 | 4913 |
| 8 | 512 | 18 | 5832 |
| 9 | 729 | 19 | 6859 |
| 10 | 1000 | 20 | 8000 |

## Properties of Cube

(i) A perfect cube can be expressed as a product of triplets of equal factors.

(ii) There are ten perfect cubes from 1 to 1000.

(iii) Cubes of all even natural numbers are even.

(iv) Cubes of all odd natural numbers are odd.

(v) Cubes of negative integers are negative.

(vi) The product of the cubes of two numbers is equal to the cube of their products. For any two natural numbers $a$ and $b$,

$$a^3 \times b^3 = ( a \times b )^3.$$

(vii) The cube of a rational number is the cube of its numerator divided by the cube of its denominator.

$$\left( \frac{p}{q} \right)^3 = \frac{p^3}{q^3}$$

(viii) Numbers like 1729, 4104, 13832, are known as Hardy–Ramanujan Numbers. They can be expressed as sum of two cubes in two different ways. For example,

$$1729 = 1728 + 1 = 12^3 + 1^3$$
$$1729 = 1000 + 729 = 10^3 + 9^3$$

## Cube Root

Cube root is the inverse operation of cube. In other words, cube root of a number $a$ is a number $y$ such that $y^3 = a$.

## Properties of Cube Root

For all non-negative real numbers $a$ and $b$,

(i) $\sqrt[3]{a+b} \neq \sqrt[3]{a} + \sqrt[3]{b}$

(ii) $\sqrt[3]{a-b} \neq \sqrt[3]{a} - \sqrt[3]{b}$

(iii) $\sqrt[3]{a \times b} = \sqrt[3]{a} \times \sqrt[3]{b}$

(iv) $\sqrt[3]{\dfrac{a}{b}} = \dfrac{\sqrt[3]{a}}{\sqrt[3]{b}}$

=== MATHEMATICAL OPERATION ===

The rule for simplifying mathematical expressions involving multiple operations is BODMAS. BODMAS stands for the order of operation.

| | |
|---|---|
| B | Bracket |
| O | Order (Power, Square Root etc) |
| D | Division |
| M | Multiplication |
| A | Addition |
| S | Subtraction |

## Bracket Rules

If the mathematical expression contains more than one bracket, then the order of solving the bracket is:

(i) First bracket to be removed is the line bracket or bar bracket or the vinculum "-" .

(ii) Second bracket to be removed is the common bracket ( ) .

(iii) Third bracket to be removed is the curly bracket { }.

(iv) Fourth bracket to be removed is the square bracket [ ] .

## Modulus of a Real Number

Modulus of a real number $a$ is defined as

$$|a| = \begin{cases} a & \text{if } a \geq 0 \\ -a & \text{if } a < 0 \end{cases}$$

=== PERCENTAGE ===

A percentage is a fraction whose denominator is 100.

Percentage change

$$\% \text{ Change} = \frac{\text{New Value} - \text{Original Value}}{\text{Original Value}} \times 100$$

Percentage Error

$$\% \text{ Error} = \frac{\text{Error}}{\text{Real Value}} \times 100$$

Original value

$$\text{Original Value} = \frac{\text{New Value}}{100 + \% \text{ Change}} \times 100$$

Percentage increase

$$\text{New Value} = \frac{100 + \text{Percentage Increase}}{100} \times \text{Original Value}$$

Percentage decrease

$$\text{New Value} = \frac{100 - \text{Percentage Decrease}}{100} \times \text{Original Value}$$

## Relation Between Fraction, Decimal and Percent

| Fraction | Decimal | Percent | Fraction | Decimal | Percent |
|----------|---------|---------|----------|---------|---------|
| $\frac{1}{2}$ | 0.5 | 50% | $\frac{3}{5}$ | 0.6 | 60% |
| $\frac{2}{2}$ | 1.0 | 100% | $\frac{4}{5}$ | 0.8 | 80% |
| $\frac{1}{3}$ | $0.\bar{3}$ | $33\frac{1}{3}\%$ | $\frac{5}{5}$ | 1.0 | 100% |
| $\frac{2}{3}$ | $0.\bar{6}$ | $66\frac{2}{3}\%$ | $\frac{1}{8}$ | 0.125 | 12.5% |
| $\frac{3}{3}$ | 1.0 | 100% | – | 0.25 | 25% |
| $\frac{1}{4}$ | 0.25 | 25% | $\frac{3}{8}$ | 0.375 | 37.5% |
| $\frac{2}{4}$ | 0.5 | 50% | $\frac{4}{8}$ | 0.5 | 50% |

| $\frac{3}{4}$ | 0.75 | 75% | $\frac{5}{8}$ | 0.625 | 62.5% |
|---|---|---|---|---|---|
| $\frac{4}{4}$ | 1.0 | 100% | $\frac{6}{8}$ | 0.75 | 75% |
| $\frac{1}{5}$ | 0.2 | 20% | $\frac{7}{8}$ | 0.875 | 87.5% |
| $\frac{2}{5}$ | 0.4 | 40% | $\frac{8}{8}$ | 1.0 | 100% |

## Conversion of Fraction or Decimal into Percentage and Vice Versa

To convert a fraction or decimal into percentage, multiply it by 100.

For example, $\frac{4}{5} \times 100 = 80\%$

To convert a percentage into fraction or decimal, divide it by 100.

For example, 38.9 % is same as $38.9 \div 100 = 0.389$

## PROFIT AND LOSS

**Cost Price :** The price, at which an article is purchased, is called its cost price, *C.P.*

**Selling Price :** The price, at which an article is sold, is called its selling price, *S.P.*

**Profit or Gain :** If S.P. is greater than C.P., the seller is said to have a profit or gain.

**Loss :** If S.P. is less than C.P., the seller is said to have incurred a loss.

## Key Terms and Formulae

(i)  Gain = (S.P.) - (C.P.)

(ii) Loss = (C.P.) - (S.P.)

(iii) Loss or gain is always calculated on C.P.

(iv) Gain Percentage: (Gain%)

$$\text{Gain}\% = \left( \frac{\text{Gain} \times 100}{\text{C.P.}} \right)$$

(v)  Loss Percentage: (Loss%)

$$\text{Loss}\% = \left( \frac{\text{Loss} \times 100}{\text{C.P.}} \right)$$

(vi) Selling Price: (S.P.)

$$SP = \left[ \frac{(100 + Gain\%)}{100} \times C.P. \right]$$

(vii) Selling Price: (S.P.)

$$SP = \left[ \frac{(100 - Loss\%)}{100} \times C.P. \right]$$

(viii) Cost Price: (C.P.)

$$C.P. = \left[ \frac{100}{(100 + Gain\%)} \times SP \right]$$

(ix) Cost Price: (C.P.)

$$C.P. = \left[ \frac{100}{(100 - Loss\%)} \times S.P. \right]$$

(x) If a trader professes to sell his goods at cost price, but uses false weights, then

$$Gain\% = \left[ \frac{Error}{(True\ Value) - (Error)} \times 100 \right] \%$$

=== **SALES TAX AND DISCOUNT** ===

## Marked Price

The printed price of an article is called its marked price or list price (MP).

## Discount

Discount is a reduction given on marked price.

Discount = Marked Price – Sale Price.

Discount can be calculated when discount percentage is given.

Discount = Discount % of Marked Price

$$Discount\% = \frac{Discount}{MP} \times 100$$

where MP is the marked price.

## Net Selling Price

The difference between the marked price and the discount is called the net selling price (SP).

SP = Marked Price – Discount

## Banker's Discount

Banker's Discount is the difference between the value shown on a bond, share etc that is bought by a bank from a customer, and the amount that the customer actually receives from the bank. The banker's discount is kept by the bank as a payment. Thus, Banker's Discount is the simple interest on the face value for the period from the date on which the bill was discounted and the legally due date.

## Bill of Exchange

A written order by one party (the drawer) to another (the drawee) to pay a certain sum either immediately (a sight bill) or on a fixed date (a term bill) for payment of goods or services received. The drawee accepts the bill by signing it.

## Nominally Due Date

The exact date to which the bill of exchange is due for payment is known as nominally due date.

## Legally Due Date

Three days (grace days) after the nominally due date is known as legally due date.

*Note*: When the date of the bill is not given, grace days are not to be added.

## Key Terms and Formulae

(i) Banker's Discount = Simple Interest on the face value of the bill for unexpired time

$$= \frac{\text{Face Value} \times \text{Rate} \times \text{Time}}{100}$$

(ii) Banker's Gain = Banker's Discount – True Discount (for unexpired time)

$$= \text{Simple interest on True Discount}$$

$$= \frac{(\text{True Discount})^2}{\text{Present Worth}}$$

(iii) True Discount $= \sqrt{\text{Present Worth} \times \text{Banker's Gain}}$

(iv) True Discount = Simple Interest on the present worth for unexpired time

$$= \frac{\text{Present Worth} \times \text{Time} \times \text{Rate}}{100}$$

$$= \frac{\text{Face Value} \times \text{Rate} \times \text{Time}}{100 + (\text{Rate} \times \text{Time})}$$

(v) Face Value $= \dfrac{\text{Banker's Discount} \times \text{True Discount}}{\text{Banker's Discount} - \text{True Discount}}$

(vi) Present Worth = Face Value – True Discount

(vii) True Discount = $\dfrac{\text{Banker's Gain} \times 100}{\text{Rate} \times \text{Time}}$

(viii) Present Worth = $\dfrac{\text{Face Value}}{1 + \text{Time}\left(\dfrac{\text{Rate}}{100}\right)}$

## Sales Tax

Sales tax is charged on the sale of an item by the government and is added to the Bill Amount. Indian government has a fixed VAT (Value Added Tax) rate for various categories of items.

Sales tax = Tax% of Bill Amount

*Note:* If both discount and sales tax are given in a problem, then the discount is calculated first.

# ═══════ALLIGATION AND MIXTURE═══════

## Alligation

It is the rule that enables us to find the ratio in which two or more ingredients at the given price must be mixed to produce a mixture of desired price.

## Mean Price

The cost of a unit quantity of the mixture is called the mean price.

## Rule of Alligation

If two ingredients are mixed, then

$$\left(\frac{\text{Quantity of cheaper}}{\text{Quantity of dearer}}\right) = \left(\frac{\text{C.P. of dearer} - \text{Mean Price}}{\text{Mean price} - \text{C.P. of cheaper}}\right)$$

It can be represented as:

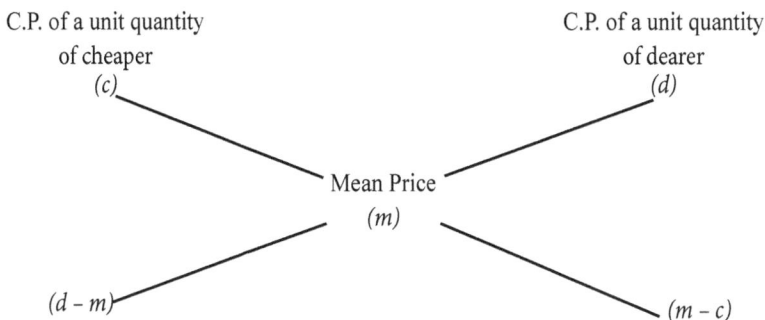

C.P. of a unit quantity of cheaper (c)

C.P. of a unit quantity of dearer (d)

Mean Price (m)

(d – m)

(m – c)

Hence, (Cheaper quantity) : (Dearer quantity) = $(d - m) : (m - c)$.

Suppose, a container contains $x$ units of liquid from which $y$ units are taken out and replaced by water.

After $n$ operations the quantity of pure liquid

$$= \left[ x \left( 1 - \frac{y}{x} \right)^n \right] \text{units.}$$

## Mixture of More Than Two Elements

(i) If $n$ different vessels of equal size are filled with the mixture of P and Q in the ratio $p_1 : q_1, p_2 : q_2, ..., p_n : q_n$ and content of all these vessels are mixed in one large vessel, then

$$\frac{\text{Quantity of P}}{\text{Quantity of Q}} = \frac{\dfrac{p_1}{p_1+q_1} + \dfrac{p_2}{p_2+q_2} + ... + \dfrac{p_n}{p_n+q_n}}{\dfrac{q_1}{p_1+q_1} + \dfrac{q_2}{p_2+q_2} + ... + \dfrac{q_n}{p_n+q_n}}$$

(ii) If $n$ different vessels of sizes $x_1, x_2, ..., x_n$ are filled with the mixture of P and Q in the ratio $p_1 : q_1, p_2 : q_2, ..., p_n : q_n$ and content of all these vessels are mixed in one large vessel, then

$$\frac{\text{Quantity of P}}{\text{Quantity of Q}} = \frac{\dfrac{p_1 x_1}{p_1+q_1} + \dfrac{p_2 x_2}{p_2+q_2} + ... + \dfrac{p_n x_n}{p_n+q_n}}{\dfrac{q_1 x_1}{p_1+q_1} + \dfrac{q_2 x_2}{p_2+q_2} + ... + \dfrac{q_n x_n}{p_n+q_n}}$$

(iii) If a vessel contains 'x' litres of liquid A and if 'y' litres be withdrawn and replaced by liquid B, and the operation is repeated 'n' times in all, then :

$$\frac{\text{Quantity of liquid A after } n^{th} \text{ operation}}{\text{Initial quantity of liquid of A}} = \left[ \frac{x-y}{x} \right]^n = \left[ 1 - \frac{y}{x} \right]^n$$

(iv) $p$ gram of an ingredient solution has $a\%$ ingredient in it. To increase the ingredient content to $b\%$ in the solution

$$\text{Quantity of ingredient need to be added} = \frac{p(b-a)}{100-b}$$

# INTEREST

**Principal :** The money borrowed is known as principal.

**Rate :** The percentage of a sum of money which is charged or paid for the use of money is known as rate of interest.

**Interest :** The extra money which is paid for using the principal is known as interest.

$$\text{Simple Interest} = \frac{\text{Principal} \times \text{Rate} \times \text{Time}}{100}$$

Amount = Principal + Simple Interest

**Compound Interest :** The interest earned on capital when the interest is periodically added to the principal.

If P = Principal, R = Rate, T = Time

When Compound Interest reckoned

*(i)* **Annually**

$$\text{Amount} = P \left\{ 1 + \frac{R}{100} \right\}^{T}$$

*(ii)* **Half-Yearly**

$$\text{Amount} = P \left\{ 1 + \frac{R}{2 \times 100} \right\}^{2 \times T}$$

*i.e.* Rate = R/2 and Time = $2 \times T$

*(iii)* **Quarterly**

$$\text{Amount} = P \left\{ 1 + \frac{R}{4 \times 100} \right\}^{4 \times T}$$

*i.e.* Rate = R/4 and Time = $4 \times T$

*(iv)* If Principal = P, Rate = $r_1$ % for 1st year, $r_2$ % for 2nd year, $r_3$ % for 3rd year and so on and in the last $r_n$ % for $n$th year

$$\text{Amount} = P \left\{ \left(1 + \frac{r_1}{100}\right)\left(1 + \frac{r_2}{100}\right)\left(1 + \frac{r_3}{100}\right) \dots \left(1 + \frac{r_n}{100}\right) \right\}$$

*(v)* If Principal = P, Rate = R and Time = $a\dfrac{b}{c}$ *i.e.* Time is in fraction.

$$\text{Amount} = P\left(1 + \frac{R}{100}\right)^{a}\left(1 + \frac{R}{100} \times \frac{b}{c}\right)$$

*(vi)* Compound Interest = $P\left[\left(1 + \dfrac{R}{100}\right)^{T} - 1\right]$

## RATIO AND PROPORTION

### Ratio

A ratio is a comparison between two numbers or between two quantities with the same units. For example, the ratio of two numbers $a$ and $b$ is the fraction $\dfrac{a}{b}$, usually expressed in the lowest term. The order in which two quantities are taken to find the ratio is important.

### Equivalent Ratio

Two ratios can be compared by converting them to like fractions. If the two fractions are equal, the two given ratios are equivalent.

### Proportion

A proportion is an equation which states that two ratios are equal i.e. *a:b :: c:d*. The order of the terms is important in proportion.

In a proportion, the outermost terms are known as *extremes* and the inner two terms are known as *means*.

Also, the product of extremes = the product of means

Or, *ad = bc*.

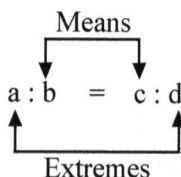

Means

a : b  =  c : d

Extremes

## TIME AND WORK

### Work from Days

If A can do a piece of work in $n$ days, then A's 1 day's work is $\dfrac{1}{n}$.

### Days from Work

If A's 1 day's work is $\dfrac{1}{n}$, then A can finish the work in $n$ days.

## Ratio of Work Done

If A is twice as good a workman as B, then:

Ratio of work done by A and B = 2 : 1

Ratio of time taken by A and B to finish a work = 1 : 2

## Key Terms and Formulae

(i) If A can do a piece of work in $a$ days and B can do the same piece of work in $b$ days by working alone, then A and B together can finish the work in $\dfrac{ab}{a+b}$ days

(ii) If A, B and C can complete a piece of work in $a$, $b$ and $c$ days respectively by working alone, then they will together complete the work in $\dfrac{abc}{ab+bc+ca}$ days

(iii) If A and B working together can finish a piece of work in $p$ days, A working alone can finish in $q$ days, then B working alone will finish the work in $\dfrac{pq}{q-p}$ days

(iv) A and B working together can finish a piece of work in $p$ days, B and C working together can finish a piece of work in $q$ days and C and A working together can finish a piece of work in $r$ days then

a) A, B and C working together can finish the work in $\dfrac{2pqr}{pq+qr+rp}$ days

b) A alone can finish the work in $\dfrac{2pqr}{pq+qr-rp}$ days

c) B alone can finish the work in $\dfrac{2pqr}{qr+rp-pq}$ days

(v) If A working alone takes $a$ days more than A and B working together, B working alone takes $b$ days more than A and B working together then the time taken by A and B to complete the work is equal to:
$\sqrt{ab}$ days

(vi) If $a$ men and $b$ women can complete a piece of work in $n$ days then $c$ men and $d$ women will complete the same work in $\dfrac{nab}{bc+ad}$ days

(vii) Let two groups of people have the same efficiency. If $M_1$ men can do $W_1$ work in $D_1$ days working $H_1$ hours per day and if $M_2$ men can do $W_2$ work in $D_2$ days working $H_2$ hours per day, then:

$$\frac{M_1 D_1 H_1}{W_1} = \frac{M_2 D_2 H_2}{W_2}$$

**Inlet :** A pipe connected with a reservoir or a tank or a cistern that fills it, is known as an inlet.

**Outlet :** A pipe connected with a reservoir or a tank or a cistern that empties it, is known as an outlet.

## Filling and Emptying of Pipe

(i) If a pipe can fill a tank in $x$ hours, then the part filled in 1 hour $= \dfrac{1}{x}$.

(ii) If a pipe can empty a tank in $y$ hours, then the part emptied in 1 hour $= \dfrac{1}{y}$.

(iii) If a pipe can fill a tank in $x$ hours and another pipe can empty the full tank in $y$ hours (where $y > x$), then on opening both the pipes the part emptied in 1 hour $= \dfrac{1}{y} - \dfrac{1}{x}$

(iv) If a pipe can fill a tank in $x$ hours and another pipe can empty the full tank in $y$ hours (where $y > x$), then on opening both the pipes the part filled in 1 hour $= \dfrac{1}{x} - \dfrac{1}{y}$

(v) If $x$ is the time taken to fill a container and $y$ is the time taken to fill the same container due to leak, then total time taken to fill the container $= \dfrac{xy}{y - x}$

(vi) Let $x$ be the time taken to fill a container by pipe X and $y$ be the time taken to fill a container by pipe Y while working alone. If both the pipes are opened together then, time taken to fill the container $= \dfrac{xy}{x + y}$

(vii) Let there be three inlet pipes X, Y and Z. Let $x$, $y$, and $z$ be the time taken to fill the containers X, Y and Z respectively while working alone. If all the three pipes are opened together, then time taken to fill the container

$$= \frac{xyz}{xy + yz + zx}$$

(viii) Let there be two inlet pipes X and Y and one outlet pipe Z. If x is the time taken to fill a container by pipe X, y is the time taken to fill a container by pipe Y and z is the time taken to fill a container when all the pipes are open, then time taken to empty the container

$$= \frac{xyz}{xz + yz - xy}$$

(ix) If $d_1, d_2$ and $d_3$ be the diameters of three pipes filling a container where $d_1 > d_2 > d_3$, then the total time required to fill the container when all the pipes are open is given by

$$\text{Time required} = \left[\frac{(\text{Time taken by largest pipe}) \times d_1^2}{d_1^2 + d_2^2 + d_3^2}\right]$$

(x) If an inlet pipe X is k times faster and takes $x$ minutes less time than inlet pipe Y then

a) the time taken to fill a container if both pipes are opened together is given by $= \dfrac{kx}{(k-1)^2}$

b) Time taken by X to fill the container $= \dfrac{x}{k-1}$

c) Time taken by Y to fill the container $= \dfrac{kx}{k-1}$

## CLOCKS AND CALENDAR

## Minute Space
For calculation purpose, the dial of a clock is taken as a circle whose circumference is divided into 60 equal parts, known as minute space.

## Hour Hand and Minute Hand
A clock has two hands. The smaller hand is called the hour hand while the larger one is called the minute hand.

## Properties of a Clock
(i) There are 360 degrees of angular measurement in a circle. This is applied to the clock problem because a standard non-digital clock is generally a circle.

(ii) The angle between two consecutive hours is 30 degrees.

(iii) The angle between two consecutive minutes is 6 degrees.

(vi) In every hour, both the hands coincide once.

(v) The hands are in the same straight line when they are coincident or opposite to each other.

(vi) When the two hands are at right angles, they are 15 minute spaces apart.

(vii) Angle traced by hour hand in 12 hours = 360°

(viii) Angle traced by minute hand in 60 minutes = 360°

(ix) If a clock shows 7.20, when the correct time is 7, it is said to be 20 minutes too fast.

x) On the other hand, if it indicates 7.40, when the correct time is 8, it is said to be 20 minutes too slow.

## Properties of a Calendar

(i)   1 week = 7 days

(ii)  1 month = 30 or 31 days (except February, for calculation purpose 30 is taken unless the name of the month is mentioned).

(iii) A period of ten years is known as a decade.

(iv)  A period of 100 years is known as a century.

(v)   The first day of a century is either Monday, Tuesday, Thursday or Saturday.

(vi)  The last day of a century cannot be Tuesday, Thursday or Saturday.

(vii) An ordinary year has 365 days (February = 28 days)

(viii)A leap year has 366 days (February = 29 days)

(ix)  A leap year comes once in four years.

(x)   The year which is divisible by four is a leap year, if it is not a century. For a century to be a leap year it should be divisible by 400.

(xi)  Every 4th century is a leap year and no other century is a leap year. For example, 2000 is a leap year but 2100 is not a leap year.

(xii) There are 52 weeks in a year.

## Odd Days

The number of days more than the complete weeks are called odd days.

| | | |
|---|---|---|
| 1 Ordinary year | = | 52 Weeks + 1 odd day |
| 1 Leap year | = | 52 Weeks + 2 odd days |
| 1 Century | = | 76 Ordinary years + 24 Leap years |
| | = | 76 Odd days + 48 Odd days |
| | = | 124 Odd days |
| | = | 17 weeks + 5 odd days |

| Number of odd days | 0 | 1 | 2 | 3 | 4 | 5 | 6 |
|---|---|---|---|---|---|---|---|
| Day of the week | Sunday | Monday | Tuesday | Wednesday | Thursday | Friday | Saturday |

## Working Rule When No Reference Day is Given

To find the day of the week on a particular date when no reference day is given

(i)  Count the total number of odd days on the given date.

(ii) Use the above table to find out the day of the week.

## Working Rule when Reference Day is Given

To find the day of the week on a particular date when a reference day is given

(i) Count the total number of odd days for the period between the given date and the reference date. (Include the given date but exclude the reference date during counting).

(ii) The day of the week on the particular date is equal to the total number of odd days behind the reference date if the given date was behind the reference date and ahead of the reference date if the reference date was ahead of it.

## ═══════ SPEED, DISTANCE AND TIME ═══════

## Key Terms and Formulae

Distance = Speed × Time

$$\text{Speed} = \frac{\text{Distance}}{\text{Time}}$$

(i) In a race if P is $n$ times as fast as Q and Q starts $x$ metres ahead of P, then length of the race course so that both P and Q reach the finishing line at the same time is

$$x\left(\frac{n}{n+1}\right) \text{meters}$$

(ii) If P can run $p$ metres race in $t_1$ seconds and Q in $t_2$ seconds where $t_1 < t_2$ then P beats Q by a distance $= \dfrac{p}{t_2} \times (t_2 - t_1)$

(iii) If P covers a distance $d_1$ km at $s_1$ km/h and then $d_2$ km at $s_2$ km/h, then the average speed during the whole journey is

$$\frac{s_1 s_2 (d_1 + d_2)}{s_1 d_2 + s_2 d_1} km/h$$

(iv) If P goes from A to B at $s_1$ km/h and returns from B to A at $s_2$ km/h, then the average speed during the whole journey is

$$\frac{2 s_1 s_2}{s_1 + s_2} km/h$$

(v) If a man covers a certain distance at $x$ km/h and an equal distance at $y$ km/h and $z$ km/h, then the average speed during the whole journey is $= \dfrac{3xyz}{(xy + yz + zx)} km/h$

(vi)  If a body travels distance $d_1$, $d_2$, ... in time $t_1$, $t_2$, ... respectively then

$$\text{Average Speed} = \frac{\text{Total distance}}{\text{Total time}}$$

(vii) If the new speed of a body is $a/b$ times the original speed then the change in time to cover the same distance is

$$\left(\frac{b}{a} - 1\right) \times \text{original time.}$$

(viii) If a body moves with speed $s_1$ km/h and covers a distance $d$ km in time $t_1$ and then moves with speed $s_2$ km/h and covers the same distance in time $t_2$ then

$$\frac{\text{Product of speed}}{d} = \frac{s_1}{t_1} = \frac{s_2}{t_2} = \frac{\text{Difference of speed}}{\text{Difference of time}}$$

(ix) If the speed of the boat be $x$ km/h and the speed of the stream be $y$ km/h, then

a)  The speed of the boat upstream (direction opposite to the stream) = $(x - y)$km/h

b)  The speed of the boat downstream (direction along the stream) = $(x + y)$km/h

c)  Speed of the stream = $\frac{1}{2}$ (Down stream speed – upstream speed)

## TRAIN PROBLEMS

(i)  Time taken by a train of length $l$ metres to pass a pole or a signal post or a standing man is equal to the time taken by the train to cover $l$ metres.

(ii) Time taken by a train of length $l$ metres to pass a stationery object of length $p$ metres is the time taken by the train to cover $(l + p)$ metres.

(iii) Suppose two trains or two bodies are moving in the same direction at $u$ m/s and $v$ m/s, where $u > v$, then their relative speed is equal to $(u - v)$ m/s.

(iv) Suppose two trains or two bodies are moving in opposite directions at $u$ m/s and $v$ m/s, then their relative speed is equal to $(u + v)$ m/s.

(v)  If two trains of length $a$ metres and $b$ metres are moving in opposite directions at $u$ m/s and $v$ m/s, then the time taken by the trains to cross each other is $\frac{(a + b)}{u + v}$ sec

(vi) If two trains of length $a$ metres and $b$ metres are moving in the same directions at $u$ m/s and $v$ m/s, then the time taken by the faster train to cross the slower train is $\dfrac{(a+b)}{u-v}$ sec

(vii) If two trains (or bodies) start at the same time from points A and B towards each other and after crossing they take $a$ and $b$ sec in reaching B and A respectively, then:

$$(\text{A's speed}) : (\text{B's speed}) = (\sqrt{b} : \sqrt{a})$$

## ═══ SEQUENCE AND PROGRESSION ═══

## Sequence

An arrangement of numbers in a definite order according to some rule is known as a sequence.

Or

A function whose domain is the set of natural numbers or some subset of it of the type $\{1, 2, 3...k\}$ is known as a sequence.

### Finite Sequence

A sequence containing finite number of terms is called a finite sequence.

### Infinite Sequence

A sequence containing infinite number of terms is called an infinite sequence.

### Fibonacci Sequence

The sequence 1, 1, 2, 3, 5, 8, ... is known as Fibonacci Sequence. It is described by the following rule:

$$a_1 = a_2 = 1$$
$$a_3 = a_1 + a_2$$
$$a_n = a_{n-2} + a_{n-1}, n > 2$$

## Progression

Sequences, which follow specific patterns are called progressions.

### Arithmetic Progression (A.P)

*Definition*

An arithmetic progression (A.P.) is a sequence in which terms increase or decrease regularly by the same constant. This constant is called common difference ($d$) of the A.P.

*Standard Form of A.P*

If '$a$' is the first term and '$d$' is the common difference, then the standard form of A.P is given by

$$a, (a+d), (a+2d), (a+3d), (a+4d), ...$$

*Consecutive Terms*

For solving problems,

Three consecutive terms of an A.P are taken as

$$(a - d),\ a,\ (a + d).$$

Five consecutive terms of an A.P are taken as

$$(a - 2d),\ (a - d),\ a,\ (a + d),\ (a + 2d).$$

*General Term*

The $n^{th}$ term of the A.P. $= a_n = a + (n - 1)d$. The $n^{th}$ term is also called the general term of A.P.

*Sum of n Terms*

The sum of $n$ terms of the A.P. is

(i) $S_n = \dfrac{n}{2}\left[2a + (n - 1)d\right]$

where $a$ is the first term and $d$ is the common difference.

(ii) $S_n = \dfrac{n}{2}(a + a_n)$

where $a$ is the first term and $a_n$ is the $n^{th}$ term of the A.P .

(iii) $S_n = \dfrac{n}{2}(a + l)$

where $a$ is the first term and $l$ is the last term of the A.P.

*Note:*

- The common difference $d$ of an A.P can be negative, positive or zero.
- A.P can be finite or infinite.
- An infinite A.P does not have any last term.

*Properties of an A.P*

(i) If a constant is added or subtracted to/from each term of an A.P., the resulting sequence is also an A.P.

(ii) If each term of an A.P. is multiplied by a constant, then the resulting sequence is also an A.P.

(iii) If each term of an A.P. is divided by a non-zero constant, then the resulting sequence is also an A.P.

(iv) Three numbers $a$ , $b$, $c$ are in A.P. if $2b = a + c$

## Geometric Progression (G.P)

*Definition*

A sequence $a_1,\ a_2,\ a_3,\ ...,\ a_n$ is called geometric progression, if each term is non-zero and $\dfrac{a_{k+1}}{a_k} = r$ (constant), for $k \geq 1$

*Standard Form of G.P*

If '$a$' is the first term and '$r$' is the common ratio, then the standard form of G.P is given by $a, ar, ar^2, ar^3, \ldots$

*Consecutive Terms*

For solving problems,

Three consecutive terms of a G.P are taken as $\dfrac{a}{r}, a, ar$.

Five consecutive terms of a G.P are taken as $\dfrac{a}{r^2}, \dfrac{a}{r}, a, ar, ar^2$

*General Term*

The $n^{th}$ term of the G.P. is $a_n = ar^{n-1}$

where $a$ is the first term and $r$ is the common ratio.

*Sum of n Terms*

(i) If $r = 1$, the sum of $n$ terms is given by, $S_n = na$

(ii) If $r \neq 1$, the sum of $n$ terms of the G.P. is $S_n = a\left(\dfrac{1-r^n}{1-r}\right)$

Or,

$$S_n = a\left(\dfrac{r^n - 1}{r - 1}\right)$$

where $a$ is the first term, $r$ is the common ratio.

*Sum of Infinite Terms*

The sum of infinite number of terms of the G.P is

$$S_\infty = \sum_{n=1}^{\infty} ar^{n-1} = \dfrac{a}{1-r}, \text{ where } -1 < r < 1$$

**Properties of geometric progression**

(i) If the common ratio is:

- Negative, the terms will alternate between positive and negative.
- Positive, the terms will all be the same sign as the initial term.
- Equal to 1, the progression is a constant sequence.
- Greater than 1, there will be exponential growth towards positive or negative infinity (depending on the sign of the initial term).
- Between −1 and 1 but not zero, there will be exponential decay towards zero.
- −1, the progression is an alternating sequence

(ii) Three numbers $a, b, c$ are in G.P. if $b^2 = ac$.

**Harmonic Progression (H.P)**

The sequence $a_1, a_2, a_3 \ldots$ are said to be in Harmonic Progression if their reciprocals $\dfrac{1}{a_1}, \dfrac{1}{a_2}, \dfrac{1}{a_3} \ldots$ are in Arithmetic Progression.

## Arithmetic, Geometric and Harmonic Mean

### Arithmetic Mean

(i) If $a, b, c$ (positive numbers) are in A.P, then $b$ is called the arithmetic mean of $a$ and $c$. It is given by $b = \dfrac{a+c}{2}$

(ii) The Arithmetic Mean of $x_1, x_2, ..., x_n$ is given by

$$\text{Arithmetic Mean} = \frac{1}{n}\sum_{i=1}^{n} x_i$$

### Geometric Mean

(i) The Geometric Mean of two positive numbers $a$ and $b$ is given by

$$\text{Geometric Mean} = \sqrt{ab}$$

(ii) The Geometric Mean of $x_1, x_2, ..., x_n$ is given by

$$G = \sqrt[n]{x_1 x_2 \cdots x_n}$$

and hence

$$\log G = \frac{1}{n}\sum_{i=1}^{n} \log x_i$$

Or, the logarithm of the geometric mean is the arithmetic mean of the logarithm of numbers.

### Harmonic Mean

(i) The Harmonic Mean of two positive numbers $a$ and $b$ is given by

$$\text{Harmonic Mean} = \frac{2ab}{a+b}$$

(ii) The Harmonic Mean $H$ of the positive numbers $x_1, x_2, ..., x_n$ is defined to be the reciprocal of the arithmetic mean of the reciprocals of $x_1, x_2, ..., x_n$:

$$H = \left(\frac{1}{n} \cdot \sum_{i=1}^{n} x_i^{-1}\right)^{-1} = \frac{1}{\dfrac{1}{n} \cdot \left(\dfrac{1}{x_1} + \dfrac{1}{x_2} + \cdots + \dfrac{1}{x_n}\right)} = \frac{n}{\dfrac{1}{x_1} + \dfrac{1}{x_2} + \cdots + \dfrac{1}{x_n}}$$

# Relationship between Various Mean

## Arithmetic Mean and Geometric Mean

If $a$ and $b$ are two positive numbers then,

$$\text{Arithmetic Mean} - \text{Geometric Mean} = \frac{\left(\sqrt{a} - \sqrt{b}\right)^2}{2} \geq 0$$

Or Arithmetic Mean $\geq$ Geometric Mean

## Arithmetic, Geometric and Harmonic Mean

For positive numbers,

(i) $(\text{Geometric Mean})^2 = \text{Arithmetic Mean} \times \text{Harmonic Mean}$

(ii) Arithmetic Mean > Geometric Mean > Harmonic Mean

## Partnership

When two or more than two persons run a business jointly, they are called partners and the deal is known as partnership.

### Simple Partnership

The partnership in which the capital of each partner is invested in the business for the same time period is known as simple partnership.

### Compound Partnership

The partnership in which the capital of each partner is invested in the business for different time period is known as compound partnership.

## Working and Sleeping Partners

A partner who manages the business is known as a working partner and the partner who simply invests the money is a sleeping partner.

## Ratio of Divisions of Gains

(i) When investments of all the partners are for the same time, the gain or loss is distributed among the partners in the ratio of their investments.

Suppose A and B invest Rs. $x$ and Rs. $y$ respectively for the same time period and at the end of the given time period, the total profit is Rs P then

$$\text{A's share of profit} = \frac{x \times P}{x + y}$$

$$\text{B's share of profit} = \frac{y \times P}{x + y}$$

(ii) When investments are for different time periods, equivalent capitals are calculated for a unit of time by taking (capital × number of units of time). Now gain or loss is divided in the ratio of these capitals.

Suppose A invests Rs. $x$ for p years and B invests Rs. $y$ for q years, then

$$\frac{\text{A's share of profit}}{\text{B's share of profit}} = \frac{xp}{yq}$$

(iii) If three partners A, B and C invest capitals Rs. $x$, Rs. $y$ and Rs. $z$ for a time period of $a$, $b$ and $c$ years respectively and if P is the total profit, then

$$\text{Share of A} = \frac{axP}{ax + by + cz}$$

$$\text{Share of B} = \frac{byP}{ax + by + cz}$$

$$\text{Share of C} = \frac{czP}{ax + by + cz}$$

## Ratio of Investment Period

If three partners A, B and C invest their capitals in the ratio of $x : y : z$ and earn profits in the ratio $p : q : r$ then,

$$\text{Ratio of time of Investment of A, B, C} = \frac{p}{x} : \frac{q}{y} : \frac{r}{z}$$

## Ratio of Capital

If three partners A, B and C earn profits in the ratio of $p : q : r$ when the capital is invested for a time period of $a : b : c$ then,

$$\text{Ratio of invested capital of A, B, C} = \frac{p}{a} : \frac{q}{b} : \frac{r}{c}$$

# STOCKS AND SHARES

## Stock Capital

The total amount of money needed to run the company is called the stock capital.

## Shares or Stock

The whole capital is divided into small units, called shares or stock.

For each investment, the company issues a 'share-certificate', showing the value of each share and the number of shares held by a person.

The person who subscribes in shares or stock is called a share holder or stock holder.

## Dividend

The annual profit distributed among share holders is called dividend.

Dividend is paid annually as per share or as a percentage.

## Face Value

The value of a share or stock printed on the share-certificate is called its Face Value or Nominal Value or Par Value.

## Market Value

The stock of different companies are sold and bought in the open market through brokers at stock-exchanges. A share or stock is said to be:

   (i)  At premium or above par, if its market value is more than its face value.

   (ii)  At par, if its market value is the same as its face value.

   (iii) At discount or below par, if its market value is less than its face value.

Thus, if a Rs. 100 stock is quoted at premium of 15, then market value of the stock = Rs.(100 + 15) = Rs. 115

Likewise, if a Rs. 100 stock is quoted at a discount of 6, then market value of the stock = Rs. (100 - 6) = Rs. 94

## Brokerage

The broker's charge is called brokerage.

(i) When stock is purchased, brokerage is added to the cost price.

(ii) When stock is sold, brokerage is subtracted from the selling price.

*Points to Remember*:

- The face value of a share always remains the same.
- The market value of a share changes from time to time.
- Dividend is always paid on the face value of a share.
- Number of shares held by a person

$$\frac{\text{Total Investment}}{\text{Investment in one share}} = \frac{\text{Total Income}}{\text{Income from one share}} = \frac{\text{Total Face Value}}{\text{Face of one share}}$$

# $\textcircled{2}$ Algebra Formulae

## SURDS AND INDICES

### Law of Indices

If $x$ and $y$ are two positive real numbers and $n$ and $m$ are two positive integers $(n > m)$ then,

(i) $\dfrac{x^n}{x^m} = x^{n-m}$

(ii) $x^n x^m = x^{n+m}$

(iii) $x^n y^n = (xy)^n$

(iv) $\left[\dfrac{x}{y}\right]^n = \dfrac{x^n}{y^n}$

(v) $\left[\dfrac{x}{y}\right]^{-n} = \left[\dfrac{y}{x}\right]^n$

(vi) $x^{-n} = \dfrac{1}{x^n}$

(vii) $(x^y)^z = x^{(y \times z)}$

(viii) $x^0 = 1$

### Definition of Surd

An irrational $n$th root (square, cube or higher) which cannot be expressed as a common fraction is known as surd.

If $a$ is a positive rational number and $n$ is a positive integer such that

$a^{\frac{1}{n}} = \sqrt[n]{a}$ , then

(i) $\sqrt[n]{a}$ is called surd or radical.

(ii) $n$ is called the order of the surd.

(iii) $a$ is called the radicand.

### Law of Surds

For positive real numbers $x$, $y$, $a$, $b$ and natural numbers $m$ and $n$ :

(i) $\sqrt{x} \times \sqrt{y} = \sqrt{xy}$

(ii) $\sqrt{x} \times \sqrt{x} = x$

(iii) $\sqrt{\dfrac{x}{y}} = \dfrac{\sqrt{x}}{\sqrt{y}}$

(iv) $\left[\sqrt{x}\right]^n = \sqrt{x^n}$

(v) $\sqrt[m]{x^n} = x^{\frac{n}{m}}$

(vi) $a\sqrt{c} + b\sqrt{c} = (a+b)\sqrt{c}$

(vii) $\sqrt{a} + \sqrt{b} \ne \sqrt{a+b}$

(viii) $\sqrt{a} + \sqrt{a} = 2\sqrt{a}$

(ix) $a\sqrt{c} - b\sqrt{c} = (a-b)\sqrt{c}$

(x) $\left(\sqrt{a} + \sqrt{b}\right)\left(\sqrt{a} - \sqrt{b}\right) = a - b$

(xi) $\left(a + \sqrt{b}\right)\left(a - \sqrt{b}\right) = a^2 - b$

(xii) $a^{\frac{x}{y}} = \sqrt[y]{a^x}$

(xiii) $\left(\sqrt[n]{a}\right)^n = a$

(xiv) If $a^m = b^m$, then $a = b$

(xv) If $a^m = a^n$, then $m = n$

*Note:* If $x$ and $y$ are negative real numbers, then $\sqrt{x} \times \sqrt{y} \ne \sqrt{xy}$

## Rationalizing Surd

Rationalizing the surd is the process of getting rid of the surd in the denominator of a fraction.

- To rationalize, we multiply the numerator and denominator by a fraction which equals one.
- To rationalize fractions in the form $\sqrt{\dfrac{1}{a}}$, multiply the numerator and denominator by $\sqrt{a}$
- To rationalize fractions in the form $\dfrac{1}{a+\sqrt{b}}$, multiply the numerator and denominator by $a - \sqrt{b}$
- To rationalize fractions in the form $\dfrac{1}{a-\sqrt{b}}$, multiply the numerator and denominator by $a + \sqrt{b}$

=== VARIATION ===

## Direct Proportion

Two quantities $x$ and $y$ are said to be in direct proportion if they increase (decrease) together in such a manner that the ratio of their corresponding values remains constant.

In other words two quantities $x$ and $y$ vary directly if $\dfrac{x}{y} = k$ where $k$ is a positive number.

If $y_1$, $y_2$ are the values of $y$ corresponding to the values $x_1$, $x_2$ of $x$ respectively, then $\dfrac{x_1}{y_1} = \dfrac{x_2}{y_2}$

*Note:* When two quantities $x$ and $y$ are in direct proportion (or vary directly) they are also written as $x \propto y$.

## Inverse Proportion

Two quantities $x$ and $y$ are said to be in inverse proportion if an increase in $x$ causes a proportional decrease in $y$ (and vice-versa) in such a manner that the product of their corresponding values remains constant.

That is, if $xy = k$, then $x$ and $y$ are said to vary inversely.

If $y_1$, $y_2$ are the values of $y$ corresponding to the values $x_1$, $x_2$ of $x$ respectively, then

$x_1 y_1 = x_2 y_2$ or $\dfrac{x_1}{x_2} = \dfrac{y_2}{y_1}$

Note: When two quantities $x$ and $y$ are in inverse proportion (or vary indirectly) they are also written as $x \propto \dfrac{1}{y}$ .

=========== **POLYNOMIAL** ===========

## Polynomial

A polynomial *p(x)* in one variable $x$ is an algebraic expression in $x$ of the form

$$p(x) = a_n x^n + a_{n-1} x^{n-1} + \cdots + a_2 x^2 + a_1 x + a_0 ,$$

where $a_0, a_1, a_2, \ldots, a_n$ are constants and $a_n \neq 0$.

$a_0, a_1, a_2, \ldots, a_n$ are respectively the coefficients of $x^0, x^1, x^2, \ldots, x^n$, and '$n$' is known as the degree of the polynomial. Each of $a_n x^n$, ..., $a_0 x^0$ is called a term of the polynomial.

A polynomial has a finite number of terms.

**Monomial :** A polynomial of one term is called a monomial.

**Binomial :** A polynomial of two terms is called a binomial.

**Trinomial :** A polynomial of three terms is called a trinomial.

## Linear Polynomial

A polynomial of degree one is called a linear polynomial.

- The zero of a linear polynomial $ax + b = 0$ is given by

$$\frac{-b}{a} = \frac{-(\text{Constant term})}{\text{Coefficient of } x}$$

- For a linear polynomial $ax + b$, $a \neq 0$, the graph of $y = ax + b$ is a straight line which intersects the $x$-axis at exactly one point, $\left(\dfrac{-b}{a}, 0\right)$.

Therefore, the linear polynomial $ax + b$, $a \neq 0$, has exactly one zero, the $x$-coordinate of the point where the graph of $y = ax + b$ intersects the $x$-axis.

## Quadratic Polynomial
A polynomial of degree two is called a quadratic polynomial.
- A quadratic polynomial in $x$ with real coefficients is of the form $ax^2 + bx + c$, where $a$, $b$, $c$ are real numbers with $a \neq 0$.
- A quadratic polynomial can have at most 2 zeroes. It can have either two distinct zeroes or two equal zeroes or no zero.
- If $\alpha$ and $\beta$ are the zeroes of the quadratic polynomial $ax^2 + bx + c$, then $\alpha + \beta = -\dfrac{b}{a}, \alpha\beta = \dfrac{c}{a}$
- The graph of $ax^2 + bx + c$, where $a$, $b$, $c$ are real numbers and $a \neq 0$ is a parabola.

## Cubic Polynomial
A polynomial of degree three is called a cubic polynomial.
- A cubic polynomial in $x$ with real coefficients is of the form, $ax^3 + bx^2 + cx + d = 0$ where $a$, $b$, $c$, $d$ are real numbers with $a \neq 0$.
- A cubic polynomial can have at most 3 zeroes.
- If $\alpha$, $\beta$, $\gamma$ are the zeroes of the cubic polynomial $ax^3 + bx^2 + cx + d = 0$, then

$$\alpha + \beta + \gamma = \dfrac{-b}{a},$$

$$\alpha\beta + \beta\gamma + \gamma\alpha = \dfrac{c}{a},$$

$$\text{and } \alpha\beta\gamma = \dfrac{-d}{a}$$

## Constant Polynomial
A polynomial without any variable or variable with power zero is called a constant polynomial. For example, $p(x) = 8$, $x^0 [x^0 = 1]$. The degree of a non-zero constant polynomial is zero.

### Zero polynomial
The constant polynomial 0 is called a zero polynomial. The degree of a zero polynomial is not defined.

### Zero of a polynomial
A real number '$a$' is a zero of a polynomial $p(x)$ if $p(a) = 0$. In this case, $a$ is also called a root of the equation $p(x) = 0$.

- Every linear polynomial in one variable has a unique zero.
- A non-zero constant polynomial has no zero.
- Every real number is a zero of the zero polynomial.
- The zeroes of a polynomial $p(x)$ are precisely the x-coordinates of the points, where the graph of $y = p(x)$ intersects the x-axis.

## Graph of a Polynomial

One zero

  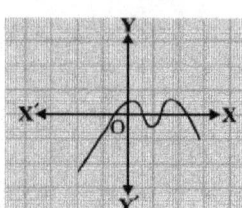

Two zeroes      Three zeroes      Four zeroes

## Division Algorithm of a Polynomial

If $p(x)$ and $g(x)$ are two polynomials such that degree of $p(x) \geq$ degree of $g(x)$ and $g(x) \neq 0$, then we can find polynomials $q(x)$ and $r(x)$ such that:

$$p(x) = g(x)q(x) + r(x),$$

where

$$r(x) = 0 \text{ or degree of } r(x) < \text{degree of } g(x).$$

Hence, $p(x)$ divided by $g(x)$ gives quotient as $q(x)$ and remainder as $r(x)$.

## Remainder Theorem

If $p(x)$ is any polynomial of degree greater than or equal to 1 and $p(x)$ is divided by the linear polynomial $x - a$, then the remainder is $p(a)$.

## Factor Theorem

$x - a$ is a factor of the polynomial $p(x)$, if $p(a) = 0$. Also, if $x - a$ is a factor of $p(x)$, then $p(a) = 0$.

# Rational Fraction

A fraction in which both the numerator and the denominator are polynomials and the denominator is not equal to zero is called a rational fraction.

## Proper Rational Fraction

If the degree of the numerator of a rational fraction is less than the degree of the denominator of the rational fraction, then that fraction is known as a proper rational fraction.

## Improper Rational Fraction

If the degree of the numerator of the rational fraction is greater than the degree of the denominator of the rational fraction, then that fraction is known as an improper rational fraction.

## Partial Fraction Expansion

Partial fraction expansion or partial fraction decomposition of a rational fraction is the proces by which the rational fraction can be expressed as a sum of a polynomial and one or more fractions with a simple denominator.

## Steps for Solving Partial Fraction

(i) If $\dfrac{P(x)}{Q(x)}$ is an improper rational function, divide $P(x)$ by $Q(x)$.

$\dfrac{P(x)}{Q(x)} = T(x) + \dfrac{R(x)}{Q(x)}$ where $T(x)$ is the quotient and $R(x)$ is the remainder.

(ii) Write $\dfrac{R(x)}{Q(x)}$ as partial fraction expansion.

(iii) Simplify.

# Partial Fraction Expansion of Some Common Rational Fractions

If A, B, C and D are real numbers then:

| S.No. | Rational Fraction | Partial Fraction Expansion |
|---|---|---|
| 1. | $\dfrac{px+q}{(x-a)(x-b)}, a \neq b$ | $\dfrac{A}{(x-a)} + \dfrac{B}{(x-b)}$ |
| 2. | $\dfrac{px+q}{(x-a)^2}$ | $\dfrac{A}{(x-a)} + \dfrac{B}{(x-a)^2}$ |
| 3. | $\dfrac{px+q}{(x-a)^3}$ | $\dfrac{A}{(x-a)} + \dfrac{B}{(x-a)^2} + \dfrac{C}{(x-a)^3}$ |
| 4. | $\dfrac{px^2+qx+r}{(x-a)(x-b)(x-c)}$ | $\dfrac{A}{(x-a)} + \dfrac{B}{(x-b)} + \dfrac{C}{(x-c)}$ |
| 5. | $\dfrac{px^2+qx+r}{(x-a)^2(x-b)}$ | $\dfrac{A}{(x-a)} + \dfrac{B}{(x-a)^2} + \dfrac{C}{(x-b)}$ |
| 6. | $\dfrac{px^2+qx+r}{(x-a)^3(x-b)}$ | $\dfrac{A}{(x-a)} + \dfrac{B}{(x-a)^2} + \dfrac{C}{(x-a)^3} + \dfrac{D}{(x-b)}$ |
| 7. | $\dfrac{px^2+qx+r}{(x-a)(x^2+bx+c)}$ | $\dfrac{A}{(x-a)} + \dfrac{Bx+C}{x^2+bx+c}$, where $x^2 + bx + c$ can not be factored further |

═══════ **ALGEBRAIC IDENTITY** ═══════

## Square of a Binomial

$(a + b)^2 = a^2 + 2ab + b^2$

$(a - b)^2 = a^2 - 2ab + b^2$

## Difference of Squares

$a^2 - b^2 = (a + b)(a - b)$

## Sum of Squares

$(a^2 + b^2) = (a + b)^2 - 2ab$

## Product of Binomials

$(x + a)(x + b) = x^2 + (a + b)x + ab$

## Cube of a Binomial

$(a + b)^3 = a^3 + 3 \cdot a^2 \cdot b + 3 \cdot a \cdot b^2 + b^3$

$(a - b)^3 = a^3 - 3 \cdot a^2 \cdot b + 3 \cdot a \cdot b^2 - b^3$

## Square of a Trinomial

$(a + b + c)^2 = a^2 + b^2 + c^2 + 2 \cdot a \cdot b + 2 \cdot b \cdot c + 2 \cdot a \cdot c$

## Sum of Cubes

$a^3 + b^3 = (a + b)(a^2 - ab + b^2)$

## Difference of Cubes

$a^3 - b^3 = (a - b)(a^2 + ab + b^2)$

## Fourth Power of a Binomial

$(a + b)^4 = (a + b)^3(a + b) = a^4 + 4a^3b + 6a^2b^2 + 4ab^3 + b^4$

## Sum of Fourth Power

$a^4 + b^4 = (a^2 - \sqrt{2} \cdot a \cdot b + b^2)(a^2 + \sqrt{2} \cdot a \cdot b + b^2)$

## Difference of Fourth Power

$a^4 - b^4 = (a^2 - b^2)(a^2 + b^2) = (a + b)(a - b)(a^2 + b^2)$

## Sum of Fifth Power

$a^5 + b^5 = (a + b)(a^4 - a^3b + a^2b^2 - ab^3 + b^4)$

## Difference of Fifth Power

$a^5 - b^5 = (a - b)(a^4 + a^3b + a^2b^2 + ab^3 + b^4)$

## Sum of n$^{th}$ Power

$a^n + b^n = (a + b)(a^{n-1} - ba^{n-2} + b^2a^{n-3} - \ldots - b^{n-2}a + b^{n-1})$

## Difference of n$^{th}$ Power

$a^n - b^n = (a - b)(a^{n-1} + ba^{n-2} + b^2a^{n-3} + \ldots + b^{n-2}a + b^{n-1})$

## Another Important Identity

$a^3 + b^3 + c^3 - 3abc = (a + b + c)(a^2 + b^2 + c^2 - ab - bc - ca)$

## ═══════ EQUALITY AND INEQUALITY ═══════

## Properties of Equality

If A and B are algebraic expressions and c is a real number then,

### Addition Property of Equality

If A = B, then A + c = B + c

## Subtraction Property of Equality
If $A = B$, then $A - c = B - c$

## Multiplication Property of Equality
If $A = B$ and $c \neq 0$, then $cA = cB$

## Division Property of Equality
If $A = B$ and $c \neq 0$, then $\dfrac{A}{c} = \dfrac{B}{c}$

*Note:*

- Multiplying or dividing both sides of an equation by zero is avoided.
- Division by zero is undefined and multiplying both sides by zero will result in an equation $0 = 0$.

## Symmetric Property
If $A = B$, then $B = A$

## Transitive Property
If $A = B$ and $B = C$, then $A = C$

## Definition of Inequality
Two real numbers or two algebraic expressions related by the symbols $<, >, \leq$ or $\geq$ form an inequality.

## Rules of Inequality

(i) Equal numbers may be added to (or subtracted from ) both sides of an inequality.

If $a > b$, then $a + c > b + c$

If $a < b$, then $a + c < b + c$

(ii) Both sides of an inequality can be multiplied (or divided ) by the same positive number.

If $a > b$ and $c > 0$, then $ac > bc$

If $a > b$ and $c > 0$, then $\dfrac{a}{c} > \dfrac{b}{c}$

(iii) When both sides of an inequality are multiplied (or divided) by a negative number, then the inequality is reversed.

If $a > b$ and $c < 0$, then $ac < bc$

If $a > b$ and $c < 0$, then $\dfrac{a}{c} < \dfrac{b}{c}$

(iv) For double inequalities:

If $a > b$ and $c > d$, then $a + c > b + d$

If $a > b$ and $c = d$, then $a + c > b + d$

If $a < b$ and $c < d$, then $a + c < b + d$

If $a < b$ and $c = d$, then $a + c < b + d$

The values of $x$, which makes an inequality a true statement, are called solutions of the inequality.

# Number Line of an Inequality

To represent $x < a$ (or $x > a$) on a number line, put a dark circle on the number on $a$ and dark line to the left (or right) of the number $a$.

$$x < a$$

To represent $x \leq a$ (or $x \geq a$) on a number line, put a dark circle on the number on $a$ and dark line to the left (or right) of the number $x$.

$$x \geq a$$

# Graph of an Inequality

- If an inequality is having $\leq$ or $\geq$ symbol, then the points on the line are also included in the solutions of the inequality and the graph of the inequality lies left (below) or right (above) of the graph of the equality represented by dark line that satisfies an arbitrary point in that part.

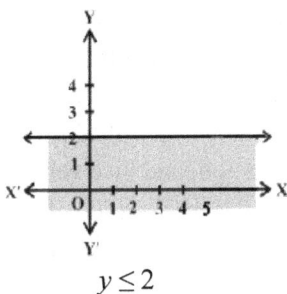

$$y \leq 2$$

- If an inequality is having $<$ or $>$ symbol, then the points on the line are not included in the solutions of the inequality and the graph of the inequality lies to the left (below) or right (above) of the graph of the corresponding equality represented by dotted line that satisfies an arbitrary point in that part.

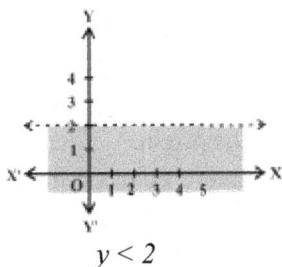

$$y < 2$$

- The region containing all the solutions of an inequality is called the solution region.

═══════ **LINEAR EQUATION** ═══════

# Equation

An equation is a statement indicating that two algebraic expressions are equal.

# Linear Equation in One Variable

A linear equation in one variable $x$ is an equation that can be written in the form $ax + b = 0$ where $a$ and $b$ are real numbers and $a \neq 0$.

## Solution of a Linear Equation

The solution of a linear equation is not affected when:

(i) the same number is added to (or subtracted from) both sides of the equation.

(ii) the same non-zero number is multiplied or divided by on both sides of the equation.

(iii) A linear equation in one variable has only one solution.

## Linear Equation in Two Variables

An equation of the form $ax + by + c = 0$, where $a$, $b$ and $c$ are real numbers, such that $a$ and $b$ both are not zero, is called a linear equation in two variables.

## Solution of Linear Equations in Two Variables

A linear equation in two variables has infinitely many solutions.

Each solution $(x, y)$ of a linear equation in two variables,

$ax + by + c = 0$, corresponds to a point on the line representing the equation, and vice versa.

$x = 0$ is the equation of the *y-axis* and $y = 0$ is the equation of the *x-axis*.

## Graph of Linear Equations in Two Variables

- The graph of every linear equation in two variables is a straight line.
- The graph of $x = a$ is a straight line parallel to the *y-axis*.
- The graph of $y = a$ is a straight line parallel to the *x-axis*.
- An equation of the type $y = mx$ represents a line passing through the origin.
- Every point on the graph of a linear equation in two variables is a solution of the linear equation. Every solution of the linear equation is a point on the graph of the linear equation.

## Pair of Linear Equations in Two Variables

Two linear equations in the same two variables are called a pair of linear equations in two variables. The most general form of a pair of linear equations is

$$a_1x + b_1y + c_1 = 0$$
$$a_2x + b_2y + c_2 = 0$$

where $a_1$, $a_2$, $b_1$, $b_2$, $c_1$, $c_2$ are real numbers, such that
$$a_1^2 + b_1^2 \neq 0, \quad a_2^2 + b_2^2 \neq 0.$$

## Solution of a pair of linear equations

A pair of linear equations in two variables can be represented and solved by the following methods.

## (a) Graphical method

The graph of a pair of linear equations in two variables is represented by two lines.

(i) If the lines intersect at a point, then that point gives the unique solution of the two equations. The pair of equations is said to be consistent in this case.

(ii) If the lines coincide, then there are infinitely many solutions — each point on the line being a solution. In this case, the pair of equations is dependent ( Dependent equations are always consistent).

(iii) If the lines are parallel, then the pair of equations has no solution. The pair of equations is said to be inconsistent in this case.

## (b) Algebraic method

Different methods for solving a pair of linear equations by algebraic methods are:

(i) *Substitution Method*

- Find the value of one variable in terms of the other variable from one of the equations (*i.e.* $x$ in terms of $y$).

- Substitute this value of the variable in the other equation, and reduce it to an equation in one variable. Solve it.

- Now substitute the value of the variable obtained in second step in the equation used in the first step to obtain the other variable.

(ii) *Elimination Method*

- Multiply both the equations by some suitable non-zero constant to make the coefficient of one of the variables numerically equal.

- Next add or subtract one equation from the other in order to eliminate one of the variables.

  If we get an equation in one variable, go to the third step.

  If in the second step, we get a true statement involving no variable, then the original pair of equations has infinitely many solutions.

  If in the second step, we get a false statement involving no variable, then the original pair of equations has no solution,

- Solve the equation in one variable.

- Substitute this value of the variable in either of the original equations to get the value of the other variable.

### (iii) Cross-multiplication Method

If a pair of linear equations is given by

$$a_1x + b_1y + c_1 = 0$$
$$a_2x + b_2y + c_2 = 0$$

then

$$x = \frac{b_1c_2 - b_2c_1}{a_1b_2 - a_2b_1}, y = \frac{c_1a_2 - c_2a_1}{a_1b_2 - a_2b_1} \text{ provided } a_1b_1 - a_2b_2 \neq 0$$

## Different Conditions

If a pair of linear equations is given by

$$a_1x + b_1y + c_1 = 0$$
$$a_2x + b_2y + c_2 = 0$$

then the following situations can arise :

(i) $\frac{a_1}{a_2} \neq \frac{b_1}{b_2}$

In this case, the pair of linear equations is consistent.

(ii) $\frac{a_1}{a_2} = \frac{b_1}{b_2} \neq \frac{c_1}{c_2}$

In this case, the pair of linear equations is inconsistent.

(iii) $\frac{a_1}{a_2} = \frac{b_1}{b_2} = \frac{c_1}{c_2}$

In this case, the pair of linear equations is consistent and dependent.

========= **AGE PROBLEMS** =========

While solving age problems, represent the following in terms of a variable:

(i) the present ages of people, animals etc.

(ii) the age at the other specified time of the people/animal involved.

Then, form an equation based on the variables as per the given conditions.

## Main Rules

(i) If the present age is $x$, then $n$ times the age is $nx$

(ii) If the present age is $x$, then age $n$ years later/hence $= x + n$

(iii) If the present age is $x$, then age $n$ years ago $= x - n$

(iv) The ages in a ratio $a : b$ will be $ax$ and $bx$

(v) If the present age is $x$, then $\frac{1}{n}$ of the age is $\frac{x}{n}$

## Standard Form of Quadratic Equation

An equation of degree two is known as a quadratic equation. The general form or standard form of a quadratic equation is $ax^2 + bx + c = 0$, where $x$ represents a variable or an unknown, and $a$, $b$, and $c$ are constants with $a \neq 0$. (If $a = 0$, the equation is reduced to a linear equation).

## Roots of a Quadratic Equation

A real number $\alpha$ is said to be a root of the quadratic equation

$$ax^2 + bx + c = 0, \text{ if } a\alpha^2 + b\alpha + c = 0,$$

- The zeroes of the quadratic polynomial $ax^2 + bx + c$ and the roots of the quadratic equation $ax^2 + bx + c = 0$ are the same.
- If we can factorise $ax^2 + bx + c$, $a \neq 0$, into a product of two linear factors, then the roots of the quadratic equation $ax^2 + bx + c = 0$ can be found by equating each factor to zero.

## Completing Square

(i) Write the quadratic equation in the standard form.

(ii) Divide each side by $a$, the coefficient of the squared term.

(iii) Rearrange the equation so that the constant term $\dfrac{c}{a}$ is on the right side.

(iv) Add the square of half of $\dfrac{b}{a}$, the coefficient of $x$, to both sides. This completes the square, converting the left side into a perfect square.

(v) Write the left side as a perfect square and simplify the right side if required.

(vi) Make two linear equations by equating the square root of the left side with the positive and negative square roots of the right side.

(vii) Solve the two linear equations.

## Quadratic Formula

The two roots of the quadratic equation $ax^2 + bx + c = 0$ are given by

$$x_1 = \frac{-b + \sqrt{b^2 - 4ac}}{2a} \ , \ x_2 = \frac{-b - \sqrt{b^2 - 4ac}}{2a} \ \text{ provided } b^2 - 4ac \geq 0.$$

$b^2 - 4ac$ is called the discriminant of the quadratic equation $ax^2 + bx + c = 0$.

## Nature of Roots

If $b^2 - 4ac > 0$, the equation has two real and distinct roots.

If $b^2 - 4ac = 0$, both the roots are real and equal.

If $b^2 - 4ac < 0$, the roots are complex conjugate.

## Graph of Quadratic Polynomial

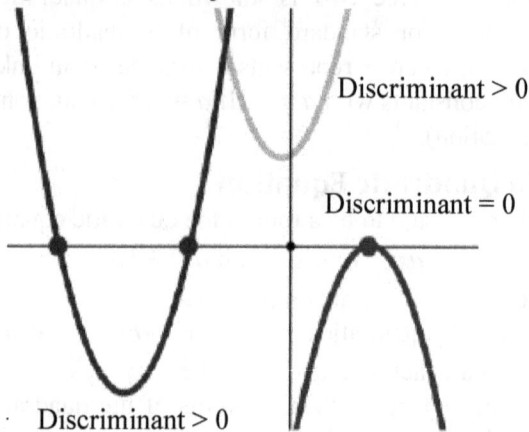

Discriminant $> 0$

Discriminant $= 0$

Discriminant $> 0$

The graph of quadratic polynomial $ax^2 + bx + c, a \neq 0$ is given by

## Sum and Product of Roots

Sum of roots of a quadratic equation $= \dfrac{-b}{a}$

Product of roots of a quadratic equation $= \dfrac{c}{a}$

When both sum and product of the roots of a quadratic equation are given, the equation is determined by using the formula:

$$x^2 - (\text{sum of roots})x + \text{Product of roots} = 0$$

=========== **COMPLEX NUMBER** ===========

## Definition

A number of the form $a + ib$, where $a$ and $b$ are real numbers, is called a complex number, $a$ is called the real part and $b$ is called the imaginary part of the complex number. A complex number is generally represented by the letter $Z$.

## Equality of Complex Numbers

Two complex numbers $a + ib$ and $c + id$ are said to be equal if $a = c$ and $b = d$.

## Sum of Complex Numbers

Let $z_1 = a + ib$ and $z_2 = c + id$. Then

$z_1 + z_2 = (a + c) + i(b + d)$

# Addition Properties of Complex Numbers

## (i) Closure Law
The sum of two complex numbers is a complex number, i.e., $z_1 + z_2$ is a complex number for all complex numbers $z_1$ and $z_2$.

## (ii) Commutative Law
For any two complex numbers $z_1$ and $z_2$, $z_1 + z_2 = z_2 + z_1$

## (iii) Associative Law
For any three complex numbers $z_1$, $z_2$ and $z_3$,
$(z_1 + z_2) + z_3 = z_1 + (z_2 + z_3)$

## (iv) Additive Identity
There exists the complex number $0 + i\ 0$, called the additive identity such that, for every complex number $z$, $z + 0 = z$

## (v) Additive Inverse
For every complex number $z = a + ib$, the complex number $-a + i(-b)$ (denoted as $-z$), is known as the additive inverse .
$$z + (-z) = 0$$

# Difference of Complex Numbers
Let $z_1 = a + ib$ and $z_2 = c + id$. Then $z_1 - z_2 = z_1 + (-z_2) = (a - c) + i(b - d)$

# Product of Complex Numbers
Let $z_1 = a + ib$ and $z_2 = c + id$. Then $z_1 z_2 = (ac - bd) + i(ad + bc)$

# Multiplication Properties of Complex Numbers

## (i) Closure Law
The product of two complex numbers is a complex number, i.e., $z_1 z_2$ is a complex number for all complex numbers $z_1$ and $z_2$

## (ii) Commutative Law
For any two complex numbers $z_1$ and $z_2$, $z_1 z_2 = z_2 z_1$

## (iii) Associative Law
For any three complex numbers $z_1$, $z_2$ and $z_3$, $(z_1 z_2) z_3 = z_1 (z_2 z_3)$

## (iv) Multiplicative Identity
There exists the complex number $1 + i\ 0$, called the multiplicative identity such that, for every complex number $z$, $z.1 = z$

## (v) Multiplicative Inverse
For any non-zero complex number $z = a + ib$ ($a \neq 0$, $b \neq 0$), there exists the complex number $\dfrac{a}{a^2 + b^2} + i\dfrac{-b}{a^2 + b^2}$ denoted by $z^{-1}$ which is known as the multiplicative inverse of $z$ such that
$(a + ib)\left(\dfrac{a}{a^2 + b^2} + i\dfrac{-b}{a^2 + b^2}\right) = 1 + i0 = 1$

### (vi) Distributive Property

For any three complex numbers $z_1$, $z_2$ and $z_3$, $z_1(z_2 + z_3) = z_1z_2 + z_1z_3$, $(z_1 + z_2)z_3 = z_1z_3 + z_2z_3$

## Quotient of Complex Numbers

Let $z_1 = a + ib$ and $z_2 = c + id$. Then if $z_2 \neq 0$, the quotient is defined by $\dfrac{z_1}{z_2} = z_1\dfrac{1}{z_2}$

## Power of i

$$i^2 = -1 \text{ and } (-i)^2 = i^2 = -1$$
$$i^3 = i^2i = (-1)i = -i$$
$$i^4 = (i^2)^2 = (-1)^2 = 1$$
$$i^5 = (i^2)^2i = (-1)^2i = i$$
$$i^{-1} = \frac{1}{i} \times \frac{i}{i} = \frac{i}{-1} = -i$$
$$i^{-2} = \frac{1}{i^2} = \frac{1}{-1} = -1$$

For any integer $k$, $i^{4k} = 1$, $i^{4k+1} = i$, $i^{4k+2} = -1$, $i^{4k+3} = -i$

## Identities in Complex Numbers

For all complex numbers $z_1 = a + ib$ and $z_2 = c + id$,

(i) $(z_1 + z_2)^2 = z_1^2 + z_2^2 + 2z_1z_2$

(ii) $(z_1 - z_2)^2 = z_1^2 - 2z_1z_2 + z_2^2$

(iii) $(z_1 + z_2)^3 = z_1^3 + 3z_1^2z_2 + 3z_1z_2^2 + z_2^3$

(iv) $(z_1 - z_2)^3 = z_1^3 - 3z_1^2z_2 + 3z_1z_2^2 - z_2^3$

(v) $z_1^2 - z_2^2 = (z_1 + z_2)(z_1 - z_2)$

## Modulus of a Complex Number

The modulus of the complex number $z = a + ib$ is denoted by $|Z|$. It is defined as

$$|z| = \sqrt{a^2 + b^2}$$

## Conjugate of a Complex Number

The conjugate of a complex number $z = a + ib$ denoted by $\bar{z}$ is given by $a - ib$.

## Relation between Multiplicative Inverse and Modulus of a Complex Number

For the complex number $z = a + ib$,

$$z^{-1} = \frac{\bar{z}}{|z|^2} \text{ or } z\bar{z} = |z|^2$$

# Properties of Modulus of Complex Number

For any two complex numbers, $z_1 = a + ib$ and $z_2 = c + id$,

(i) $|z_1 z_2| = |z_1||z_2|$

(ii) $\left|\dfrac{z_1}{z_2}\right| = \dfrac{|z_1|}{|z_2|}$ provided $|z_2| \neq 0$

(iii) $\overline{z_1 z_2} = \overline{z_1}\,\overline{z_2}$

(iv) $\overline{z_1 + z_2} = \overline{z_1} + \overline{z_2}$

(v) $\overline{z_1 - z_2} = \overline{z_1} - \overline{z_2}$

(vi) $\overline{\left(\dfrac{z_1}{z_2}\right)} = \dfrac{\overline{z_1}}{\overline{z_2}}$ provided $z_2 \neq 0$

# Argand Diagram

An Argand diagram is a plot of complex numbers as points in the Argand plane. The real part of the number is plotted along the horizontal axis ($x$-axis) and the imaginary part is plotted along the vertical axis ($y$-axis).

In the Argand plane, the modulus of the complex number $z = a + ib$ is the distance between the origin and the point $A(a, b)$.

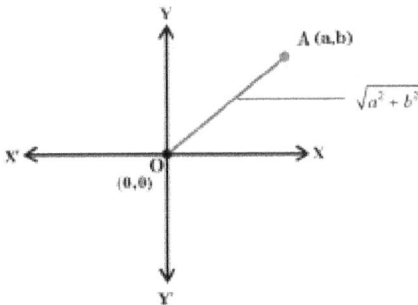

# Polar Form of a Complex Number

The polar form of the complex number $z = x + iy$ is $r(\cos\theta + i\sin\theta)$, where $r = \sqrt{x^2 + y^2}$ (the modulus of z) and $\cos\theta = \dfrac{x}{r}, \sin\theta = \dfrac{y}{r}$ ($\theta$ is the angle which the directed line segment of length $r$ makes with the positive direction of $x$ axis. It is known as the argument of z).

- For any complex number $z \neq 0$, there is only one value of $\theta$ in $0 \leq \theta < 2\pi$

- The value of $\theta$ such that $-\pi < \theta \leq \pi$ is called the principal argument of $z$

$$0 \le \theta < 2\pi$$

$$-\pi < \theta \le \pi$$

## Fundamental Theorem of Algebra

A polynomial equation has at least one root. A polynomial equation of $n$ degree has $n$ roots.

The roots of the quadratic equation $ax^2 + bx + c = 0$ $(a \ne 0)$ when $b^2 - 4ac < 0$ are given by

$$x = \frac{-b \pm \sqrt{4ac - b^2}\, i}{2a}$$

═══════════ **MATRICES** ═══════════

## Definition

A matrix is an ordered rectangular array of numbers or functions. The numbers or functions are called the elements or entries of the matrix. A matrix is denoted by a capital letter.

A matrix having $m$ rows and $n$ columns is called a matrix of order $m \times n$.

$$\begin{bmatrix} a_{11} & a_{12} & a_{13} \dots a_{1j} \dots a_{1n} \\ a_{21} & a_{22} & a_{23} \dots a_{2j} \dots a_{2n} \\ a_{r1} & a_{r2} & a_{r3} \dots a_{ij} \dots a_{in} \\ a_{m1} & a_{m2} & a_{m3} \dots a_{mj} \dots a_{mn} \end{bmatrix}_{m \times n}$$

The number of elements in $m \times n$ matrix is equal to $mn$.

## Types of matrices

### Column Matrix

A matrix is said to be a column matrix if it has only one column. $[a_{ij}]_{m \times 1}$ is a column matrix of order $m \times 1$.

## Row Matrix
A matrix is said to be a row matrix if it has only one row. $[a_{ij}]_{1 \times n}$ is a row matrix of order $1 \times n$

## Square Matrix
A matrix is said to be a square matrix if the number of rows are equal to the number of columns. An $m \times n$ matrix is a square matrix if $m = n$. It is of order $n$.

## Diagonal Matrix
A square matrix $A = [a_{ij}]_{m \times m}$ is a diagonal matrix if all its non diagonal elements are zero i.e. $a_{ij} = 0$, when $i \neq j$

## Scalar Matrix
A diagonal matrix is said to be a scalar matrix if its diagonal elements are equal. $A = [a_{ij}]_{n \times n}$ is a scalar matrix if $a_{ij} = 0$, when $i \neq j$, $a_{ij} = k$, ($k$ is some constant), when $i = j$.

## Identity Matrix
A square matrix in which the elements in the diagonal are all 1 and rest are all zero is called an identity matrix.
$A = [a_{ij}]_{n \times n}$ is an identity matrix, if $a_{ij} = 1$, when $i = j$ and $a_{ij} = 0$, when $i \neq j$.

## Zero Matrix
A zero matrix or null matrix has all its elements as zero.

# Equality of Matrices
$A = [a_{ij}] = [b_{ij}] = B$ if
 (i)  A and B are of same order,
 (ii) $a_{ij} = b_{ij}$ for all possible values of $i$ and $j$.

# Operations on Matrices
## Addition of Matrices

If $A = \begin{bmatrix} a_{11} & a_{12} & a_{13} \\ a_{21} & a_{22} & a_{23} \end{bmatrix}$ is a 2 × 3 matrix and $B = \begin{bmatrix} b_{11} & b_{12} & b_{13} \\ b_{21} & b_{22} & b_{23} \end{bmatrix}$ is another 2 × 3 matrix, then the sum of two matrices is defined by

$$A + B = \begin{bmatrix} a_{11} + b_{11} & a_{12} + b_{12} & a_{13} + b_{13} \\ a_{21} + b_{21} & a_{22} + b_{22} & a_{23} + b_{23} \end{bmatrix}$$

If $A = [a_{ij}]$ and $B = [b_{ij}]$ are two matrices of the same order, i.e. $m \times n$, then the sum of two matrices A and B is defined as a matrix $C = [c_{ij}]_{m \times n}$, where $c_{ij} = a_{ij} + b_{ij}$, for all possible values of $i$ and $j$.
*Note:* If A and B are not of the same order, then A + B is not defined.

## Multiplication of a Matrix by a Scalar

If $A = [a_{ij}]_{m \times n}$ is a matrix and $k$ is a scalar, then $kA$ is another matrix which is obtained by multiplying each element of A by the scalar $k$.

$$kA = k[a_{ij}]_{m \times n} = [k(a_{ij})]_{m \times n}$$

## Negative of a Matrix

The negative of a matrix is defined by –A.

$-A = (-1)A$

## Difference of Matrices

If $A = [a_{ij}]$, $B = [b_{ij}]$ are two matrices of the same order, i.e. $m \times n$, then the difference $A - B$ is defined as a matrix $D = [d_{ij}]$, where

$d_{ij} = a_{ij} - b_{ij}$, for all values of i and j.

In other words, $A - B = A + (-1) B$, that is sum of the matrix A and the matrix – B.

## Properties of Matrix Addition

### (i) Commutative Law

If $A = [a_{ij}]$, $B = [b_{ij}]$ are matrices of the same order, i.e. $m \times n$ , then $A + B = B + A$

### (ii) Associative Law

For any three matrices $A = [a_{ij}]$, $B = [b_{ij}]$, $C = [c_{ij}]$ of the same order, i.e. $m \times n$, $(A + B) + C = A + (B + C)$

### (iii) Existence of additive identity

Let $A = [a_{ij}]$ be an $m \times n$ matrix and O be an $m \times n$ zero matrix, then $A + O = O + A = A$. In other words, O is the additive identity for matrix addition.

### (iv) Additive Inverse

Let $A = [a_{ij}]_{m \times n}$ be any matrix, then we have another matrix as $- A = [- a_{ij}]_{m \times n}$ such that $A + (- A) = (- A) + A = O$. So – A is the additive inverse of A or negative of A.

## Properties of Scalar Multiplication of a Matrix

If $A = [a_{ij}]$ and $B = [b_{ij}]$ be two matrices of the same order, i.e. $m \times n$ and $k$ and $l$ are scalars, then

(i) $k(A + B) = kA + kB$

(ii) $(k + l)A = kA + lA$

## Product of Matrices

The product of two matrices A and B is defined if the number of columns of A is equal to the number of rows of B.

Let $A = [a_{ij}]$ be an $m \times n$ matrix and $B = [b_{jk}]$ be an $n \times p$ matrix. Then the product of the matrices A and B is the matrix C of order $m \times p$.

If $A = [a_{ij}]_{m \times n}$, $B = [b_{jk}]_{n \times p}$, then the $i^{th}$ row of A is $[a_{i1}\ a_{i2}\ ...\ a_{in}]$ and the

$k^{th}$ column of B is $\begin{bmatrix} b_{1k} \\ b_{2k} \\ \vdots \\ b_{nk} \end{bmatrix}$, then

$$c_{ik} = a_{i1}b_{1k} + a_{i2}b_{2k} + a_{i3}b_{3k} + ... + a_{in}b_{nk} = \sum_{j=1}^{n} a_{ij}b_{jk}$$

The matrix $C = [c_{ik}]_{m \times p}$ is the product of A and B.

## Properties of Matrix Multiplication

If A, B and C are $m \times n$, $n \times p$ and $m \times p$ matrices respectively, then:

### (i) Associative Law
(AB) C = A (BC), whenever both sides of the equality are defined.

### (ii) Distributive Law
    (a)  A (B + C) = AB + AC

    (b)  (A + B) C = AC + BC, whenever both sides of equality are defined.

### (iii) Existence of Multiplicative Identity
For every square matrix A, there exists an identity matrix of same order such that IA = AI = A

*Note:*
- Matrix multiplication is not always commutative i.e. AB ≠ BA even if both AB and BA are defined.
- If the product of two matrices is a zero matrix, it is not necessary that one of the matrix is a zero matrix.

## Transpose of a Matrix

If $A = [a_{ij}]$ be an $m \times n$ matrix, then the matrix obtained by interchanging the rows and columns of A is called the transpose of A. Transpose of the matrix A is denoted by $A'$ or $(A^T)$.

In other words, if $A = [a_{ij}]_{m \times n}$, then $A' = [a_{ji}]_{n \times m}$.

## Properties of Transpose of a Matrix
For any matrices A and B of suitable orders:

    (i)  $(A')' = A$,

    (ii)  $(kA)' = kA'$ where k is a constant.

    (iii) $(A + B)' = A' + B'$

    (iv) $(AB)' = B'\ A'$

## Symmetric and Skew Symmetric Matrix

If $A = [a_{ij}]$ be an $m \times n$ matrix,

    (i)  A is a symmetric matrix if $A' = A$

(ii) A is a skew symmetric matrix if $A' = -A$

## Properties of Symmetric and Skew Symmetric Matrix

(i) For any square matrix A with real number elements, $A + A'$ is a symmetric matrix and $A - A'$ is a skew symmetric matrix.

(ii) Any square matrix can be represented as the sum of a symmetric and skew symmetric matrix.

(iii) If A and B are two symmetric or skew symmetric matrices of same order, then $A + B$ also has the same order.

(iv) If A and B are two symmetric matrices of same order, then the product AB is symmetric if and only if $AB = BA$

## Elementary Matrix

A matrix is called an elementary matrix if it can be obtained from identity matrix by performing a single row or column operation.

## Row Transformations

(i) A row within the matrix can be interchanged with another row. $R_i \leftrightarrow R_j$

(ii) Each element in a row can be multiplied by a non zero constant. $R_i \rightarrow kR_i$ where $k \neq 0$.

(iii) A row can be replaced by the sum of that row and a multiple of another row. $R_i \rightarrow R_i + kR_j$ where $k$ is a constant.

## Column Transformations

(i) A column within the matrix can be interchanged with another column. $C_i \rightarrow C_j$

(ii) Each element in a column can be multiplied by a non zero constant. $C_i \rightarrow kC_i$ where $k \neq 0$.

(iii) A column can be replaced by the sum of that column and a multiple of another column. $C_i \rightarrow C_i + kC_j$ where $k$ is a constant.

## Invertible Matrix

If A and B are two square matrices such that $AB = BA = I$, then B is the inverse matrix of A denoted by $A^{-1}$ and A is the inverse of B denoted by $B^{-1}$.

- A rectangular matrix does not posses an inverse.
- Inverse of a square matrix, if it exists, is unique.
- If A and B are invertible matrices of the same order, then $(AB)^{-1} = B^{-1}A^{-1}$
- $(A^{-1})^{-1} = A$
- $(kA)^{-1} = k^{-1}A^{-1}$ for non zero scalar $k$.

## Inverse of a Matrix by Elementary Operations

### Inverse by Elementary Row Operation

(i) If A is a matrix such that $A^{-1}$ exists, then to find $A^{-1}$ by elementary row operations, write $A = IA$

Maths Formulae For School Students

(ii) Apply a series of row operations on A = IA till I = BA is obtained.

(iii) The matrix B will be the inverse of A.

## Inverse by Elementary Column Operation

(i) If A is a matrix such that $A^{-1}$ exists, then to find $A^{-1}$ by elementary column operations, write A = AI.

(ii) Apply a series of column operations on A = AI till I = AB is obtained.

(iii) The matrix B will be the inverse of A.

*Note:*

If after applying one or more elementary row (or column) operations on A = IA (A = AI), we obtain all zeros in one or more rows of the matrix A on L.H.S., then $A^{-1}$ does not exist.

## ══════════════ DETERMINANT ══════════════

## Definition

If P is the set of square matrices, Q is the set of numbers (real or complex) and $f : P \rightarrow Q$ is defined by $f(A) = k$, where $A \in P$

and $k \in Q$, then $f(A)$ is called the determinant of A. It is also denoted by det A or $|A|$ or $\Delta$

If $A = \begin{bmatrix} a & b \\ c & d \end{bmatrix}$, then $\det(A) = |A| = \begin{bmatrix} a & b \\ c & d \end{bmatrix}$

*Note:* Determinants exist only for square matrices.

## Determinant of a Matrix of Order 1

If A = [a] is a matrix of order 1, then det A = $a$

## Determinant of a Matrix of Order 2

If $A = \begin{bmatrix} a & b \\ c & d \end{bmatrix}$ is a matrix of order 2 × 2,

then $\det (A) = |A| = \begin{vmatrix} a & b \\ c & d \end{vmatrix} = ad - bc$

## Determinant of a Matrix of Order 3

If $A = \begin{bmatrix} a_1 & b_1 & c_1 \\ a_2 & b_2 & c_2 \\ a_3 & b_3 & c_3 \end{bmatrix}$ is a matrix of order 3 × 3, then

$$|A| = \begin{vmatrix} a_1 & b_1 & c_1 \\ a_2 & b_2 & c_2 \\ a_3 & b_3 & c_3 \end{vmatrix} = a_1 \begin{vmatrix} b_2 & c_2 \\ b_3 & c_3 \end{vmatrix} - b_1 \begin{vmatrix} a_2 & c_2 \\ a_3 & c_3 \end{vmatrix} + c_1 \begin{vmatrix} a_2 & b_2 \\ a_3 & b_3 \end{vmatrix}$$

*Note:* A determinant of a matrix of order 3 can be expanded in six ways (three along rows $R_1, R_2, R_3$ and three along column $C_1, C_2, C_3$).

*Note:*
- We expand the determinant along that row or column which contains maximum number of zeros.
- While expanding, we can multiply by +1 or –1 accordingly as $(i + j)$ is even or odd.
- If $A = kB$ where A and B are square matrices of order $n$, then $|A| = k^n |B|$ where $n = 1, 2, 3$

## Properties of Determinant

(i) The value of a determinant remains unchanged if its rows and columns are interchanged.

If $R_i \leftrightarrow C_i$ where $R_i$ is the $i^{th}$ row and $C_i$ is the $i^{th}$ column, then $|A|$ does not change.

(ii) If any two rows or any two columns of a determinant are interchanged, then the sign of determinant changes.

If $R_i \leftrightarrow R_j$ or $C_i \leftrightarrow C_j$, then $|A| = - |A|$

(iii) If any two rows or any two columns of a determinant are identical, then the value of the determinant is zero.

If $R_i = R_j$ or $C_i = C_j$, then $|A| = 0$

(iv) If each element of a row or each element of a column of a determinant is multiplied by a constant $k$, then the value of the determinant gets multiplied by $k$.

If $R_i \rightarrow kR_i$ or $C_i \rightarrow kC_i$ where $k \neq 0$, then $|A| = k |A|$

(v) If some or all elements of a row or column of a determinant can be expressed as sum of two or more elements, then the determinant can be expressed as the sum of two or more determinants.

(vi) If to each element of any row or column of a determinant, the equimultiples of corresponding elements of other row or column are added, then the value of the determinant remains the same.

If $R_i \rightarrow R_i + kR_j$ or $C_i \rightarrow C_i + kC_j$, then $|A|$ does not change.

## Area of a Triangle

The area of a triangle with vertices $(x_1, y_1)$, $(x_2, y_2)$ and $(x_3, y_3)$ is given by

$$\text{Area of triangle} = \frac{1}{2} \begin{vmatrix} x_1 & y_1 & 1 \\ x_2 & y_2 & 1 \\ x_3 & y_3 & 1 \end{vmatrix}$$

(i) Since area is a positive quantity, we always take the absolute value of the determinant while calculating the area.

(ii) Use both positive and negative values of the determinant for calculation when the area is given.

(iii) The area of the triangle formed by three collinear points is zero.

## Minor and Cofactor

*Minor* of an element $a_{ij}$ of a determinant is the determinant obtained by deleting its $i^{th}$ row and $j^{th}$ column in which element $a_{ij}$ lies. Minor of an element $a_{ij}$ is denoted by $M_{ij}$.

- Minor of an element of a determinant of order $n(n \geq 2)$ is a determinant of order $n - 1$.

*Cofactor* of an element $a_{ij}$ of a determinant is defined by $A_{ij} = (-1)^{i+j} M_{ij}$ where $A_{ij}$ is the cofactor and $M_{ij}$ is the minor of $a_{ij}$.

- If elements of a column are multiplied by the cofactors of any other column, then their sum is zero.
- If elements of a row are multiplied by the cofactors of any other row, then their sum is zero.

## Adjoint of a Matrix

The adjoint of a square matrix $A = [a_{ij}]_{n \times n}$ is defined as the transpose of the matrix $[A_{ij}]_{n \times n}$, where $A_{ij}$ is the cofactor of the element $a_{ij}$. Adjoint of the matrix A is represented by adjA.

If $A = \begin{vmatrix} a_{11} & a_{12} & a_{13} \\ a_{21} & a_{22} & a_{23} \\ a_{31} & a_{32} & a_{33} \end{vmatrix}$ then

$adj\ A = $ Transpose of $\begin{vmatrix} A_{11} & A_{12} & A_{13} \\ A_{21} & A_{22} & A_{23} \\ A_{31} & A_{32} & A_{33} \end{vmatrix} = \begin{vmatrix} A_{11} & A_{21} & A_{31} \\ A_{12} & A_{22} & A_{32} \\ A_{13} & A_{23} & A_{33} \end{vmatrix}$

## Property of Adjoint of a Matrix

If A be any given square matrix of order $n$, then

$A(adjA) = (adjA) A = |A| I$, where I is the identity matrix of order $n$.

## Singular and Non Sigular Matrix

A square matrix A is said to be singular if $|A| = 0$

A square matrix A is said to be non singular if $|A| \neq 0$

## Important Theorems

(i) If A and B are nonsingular matrices of the same order, then AB and BA are also nonsingular matrices of the same order.

(ii) The determinant of the product of matrices is equal to product of their respective determinants, $|AB| = |A|\ |B|$, where A and B are square matrices of the same order.

(iii) A square matrix A is invertible if and only if A is a non singular matrix.

## Inverse of a Matrix

If A is a non singular matrix, then the inverse of A is defined by

$$A^{-1} = \frac{1}{|A|} adj\, A$$

## Consistent and Inconsistent System

Consistent : A system of equations is said to be consistent if there exists one or more solution.

Inconsistent : A system of equations is said to be inconsistent if there is no solution.

## Application of Inverse of a Matrix

Let the system of equations be

$$a_1 x + b_1 y + c_1 z = d_1$$
$$a_2 x + b_2 y + c_2 z = d_2$$
$$a_3 x + b_3 y + c_3 z = d_3$$

The given system of equations can be represented as AX = B or

$$\begin{bmatrix} a_1 & b_1 & c_1 \\ a_2 & b_2 & c_2 \\ a_3 & b_3 & c_3 \end{bmatrix} \begin{bmatrix} x \\ y \\ z \end{bmatrix} = \begin{bmatrix} d_1 \\ d_2 \\ d_3 \end{bmatrix} \text{ where } A = \begin{bmatrix} a_1 & b_1 & c_1 \\ a_2 & b_2 & c_2 \\ a_3 & b_3 & c_3 \end{bmatrix}, X = \begin{bmatrix} x \\ y \\ z \end{bmatrix} \text{ and } B = \begin{bmatrix} d_1 \\ d_2 \\ d_3 \end{bmatrix}$$

## Case I

If A is a non singular matrix ($|A| \neq 0$), the inverse exists and is given by $X = A^{-1}B$. This matrix equation gives a unique solution. This method is known as *Matrix Method* of solving a system of equations.

## Case II

If A is a singular matrix, then $|A| = 0$. We calculate (adj A) B to solve the system of equations.

If (adj A) B = 0, then the system of equations may be either consistent or inconsistent and there may be infinitely many solutions or no solution.

If (adjA) B $\neq$ 0, then the solution does not exist and the system of equations is called inconsistent.

# ③ *Geometry Formulae*

=====**BASICS OF EUCLID'S GEOMETRY**=====

## Axiom and Theorem

The assumptions which are obvious universal truths are called *axioms*. They are not proved. The statements which are proved, using definitions, axioms, and deductive reasoning are called *theorems*.

## Euclid's Axioms

(i) *Transitive Property of Equality* : Things which are equal to the same thing are equal to one another.

(ii) *Addition Property of Equality* : If equals are added to equals, the wholes are equal.

(iii)*Subtraction Property of Equality* : If equals are subtracted from equals, the remainders are equal.

(iv)*Reflexive Property* : Things which coincide with one another are equal to one another.

(v) The whole is greater than the part.

## Euclid's Postulates

Postulate 1 : A straight line segment can be drawn joining any two points.

Postulate 2 : A terminated line can be produced indefinitely.

Postulate 3 : A circle can be drawn with any given point as its centre and any distance as radius.

Postulate 4 : All right angles are congruent (equal to one another).

Postulate 5 : If a straight line falling on two straight lines makes the interior angles on the same side of it taken together less than two right angles, then the two straight lines, if produced indefinitely, meet on that side on which the sum of angles is less than two right angles.

Euclid's fifth postulate can also be stated as

(i) For every line *l* and for every point P not lying on *l*, there exists a unique line *m* passing through P and parallel to *l*.

(ii) Two distinct intersecting lines cannot be parallel to the same line.

# LINE, LINE SEGMENT AND RAY

A plane is a flat surface that is infinitely large and with zero thickness.

A **line** is a group of points on a straight path that extends to infinity. It has no starting point or end point. Any two points on the line can be used to name it. This line is called line AB.

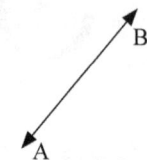

Line $AB$ ($\overleftrightarrow{AB}$)

A **line segment** is a part of a line that has two end points i.e. it has a starting point and an end point. It has a fixed length.
The two end points of the line segment are used to name the line segment. This line segment is called segment AB.

Line segment $AB$ ($\overline{AB}$)

A **ray** is a part of a line. It has one end point and extends to infinity in one direction. A ray is named starting with its end point first and then any other point on the ray.

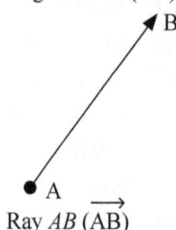

Ray $AB$ ($\overrightarrow{AB}$)

# ANGLES

## Definition
An angle is a measure of rotation of a given ray about its initial point. The initial point is known as the *vertex*. The initial ray is known as the *initial side* and the final position of the ray after rotation is called the *terminal side* of the angle.

If the direction of rotation is clockwise, then the angle is *negative* and if the direction of rotation is anticlockwise, the angle is said to be *positive*.

(a)

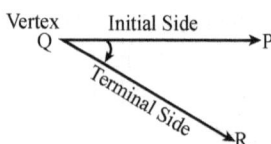

(b)

## Unit of Angle
The unit of angle is degree or radian. The angle subtended at the centre by two unit radii and an arc of length 1 unit is known as 1 radian.

## Relation between Degree and Radian

$2\pi$ Radian $= 360°$

Or $\pi$ Radian $= 180°$

Radian measure $= \dfrac{\pi}{180} \times$ Degree measure

Degree measure $= \dfrac{180}{\pi} \times$ Radian measure

1 radian $= 57° \; 17'$ approximately.

$1° = 0.017453$ radian approximately.

## Acute Angle

An angle whose measure is between $0°$ and $90°$ is called an acute angle.

## Right Angle

An angle whose measure is equal to $90°$ is called a right angle.

## Obtuse Angle

An angle whose measure is greater than $90°$ but less than $180°$ is called an obtuse angle.

## Straight Angle

An angle whose measure is equal to $180°$ is called a straight angle.

## Reflex Angle

An angle whose measure is greater than $180°$ but less than $360°$ is called a reflex angle.

## Complete Angle

One complete revolution from the position of the initial side is known as a complete angle. The measure of a complete angle is $360°$

## Adjacent Angles

Two angles are said to be adjacent if they have a common arm, a common vertex and are non overlapping.

$\angle AOB$ and $\angle BOC$ are adjacent angles. Here, OB is the common arm and O is the common vertex.

When two angles are adjacent, their sum is always equal to the angle formed by two non common arms.

$\angle AOB + \angle BOC = \angle AOC$

## Complementary Angles

Two angles are said to be complementary angles, if the sum of their measures is equal to 90°. These may be adjacent angles as well.

∠AOB and ∠BOC are adjacent angles as well as complementary angles.

∠AOB + ∠BOC = 90°

∠ABC and ∠DEF are complementary angles but not adjacent since they don't have a common arm or a common vertex.

∠ABC + ∠DEF = 90°

## Supplementary Angles

Two angles are said to be supplementary if the sum of their measures is equal to 180°. These may be adjacent angles as well.

∠AOB and ∠BOC are supplementary as well as adjacent.

∠AOB + ∠BOC = 180°

∠ABC and ∠DEF are supplementary but not adjacent.

∠ABC + ∠DEF = 180°

## Linear Pair

Two angles that are adjacent as well as supplementary are said to form a linear pair.

∠AOB and ∠ BOC form a linear pair.

∠AOB + ∠ BOC = 180°

## Vertically Opposite Angles

When two lines intersect the angles opposite to each other are known as vertically opposite angles. They are always equal.

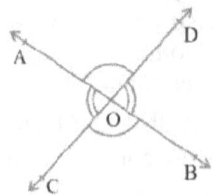

∠AOD and ∠ BOC, ∠AOC and ∠ BOD are vertically opposite angles.

∠AOD = ∠ BOC, and ∠ AOC = ∠ BOD

## Some important Axioms

(i) If a ray stands on a line, then the sum of two adjacent angles so formed is 180°.

(ii) If the sum of two adjacent angles is 180°, then the non-common arms of the angles form a straight line.

## ═PARALLEL AND PERPENDICULAR LINES═

Lines are parallel if they lie in the same plane, and are the same distance apart over their entire length.

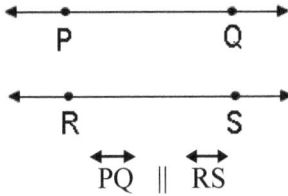

$$\overset{\longleftrightarrow}{PQ} \parallel \overset{\longleftrightarrow}{RS}$$

Two lines or line segments are said to be perpendicular if they are at right angles to each other.

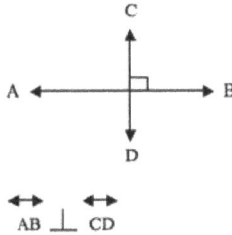

$$\overset{\longleftrightarrow}{AB} \perp \overset{\longleftrightarrow}{CD}$$

## Intersecting Lines

Two or more lines that meet at a point are called intersecting lines.

*Note*:

Two lines in a plane can either be parallel or intersecting.

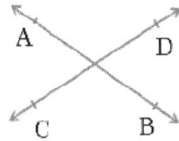

## Transversal

A line which intersects two or more lines at distinct points is known as a transversal.

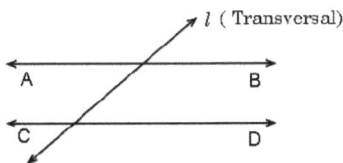

## Angles formed by Parallel Lines

If two parallel lines are intersected by a transversal, then

(i) Each pair of corresponding angles is equal.

$\angle 1 = \angle 5, \angle 2 = \angle 6, \angle 4 = \angle 8, \angle 3 = \angle 7$

(ii) Each pair of alternate interior angles is equal.

$\angle 4 = \angle 6, \angle 3 = \angle 5$

(iii) Each pair of alternate exterior angles is equal.

$\angle 1 = \angle 7, \angle 2 = \angle 8$

(iv) Each pair of interior angles on the same side of the transversal is supplementary.

$\angle 4 + \angle 5 = 180°$ and $\angle 3 + \angle 6 = 180°$

## Converse Theorems

(i) If a transversal intersects two lines such that a pair of corresponding angles is equal, then the two lines are parallel to each other.

(ii) If a transversal intersects two lines such that a pair of alternate interior angles is equal, then the two lines are parallel.

(ii) If a transversal intersects two lines such that a pair of interior angles on the same side of the transversal is supplementary, then the two lines are parallel.

## Lines Parallel to the Same Line

Lines which are parallel to the same line are parallel to each other.

$AB \parallel CD$ and $CD \parallel EF$ implies $AB \parallel EF$.

A triangle has six elements (three sides and three angles).

## Triangles Classified by Their Sides

**Scalene triangle:** A scalene triangle is a triangle that has no equal sides.

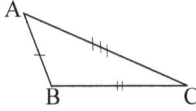

**Isosceles triangle:** An isosceles triangle is a triangle that has two equal sides.

**Equilateral triangle:** An equilateral triangle is a triangle that has three equal sides.

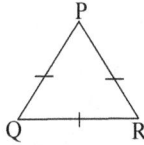

## Triangles Classified by Their Angles

### Right Angled Triangle

A right angled triangle is a triangle which has one right angle.

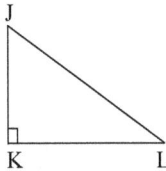

### Obtuse Angled Triangle

An obtuse angled triangle is a triangle which has one obtuse angle.

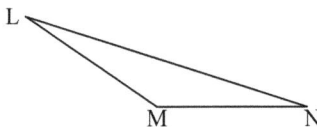

## Acute Angled Triangle

An acute angled triangle is a triangle in which all the angles are less than 90 degrees, so all the angles are acute angles.

## Naming Triangles Using Sides and Angles

- If a triangle has one right angle and two equal sides, we can call that triangle right isosceles triangle
- If a triangle has only acute angles and no equal sides, we can call that triangle acute scalene triangle.
- If a triangle has two equal sides and one obtuse angle, we can call that triangle obtuse isosceles triangle.

*Note:*

An equilateral triangle cannot have an obtuse angle or a right angle because all 3 angles in an equilateral triangle measure 60 degrees.

## Exterior Angle of a Triangle

An exterior angle of a triangle is formed when a side of a triangle is produced. At each vertex, we have two ways of forming an exterior angle.

At vertex C, angle ACD and angle BCE are the two ways of forming an exterior angle.

## Median, Altitude and Perpendicular bisector of a Triangle

**Median of a triangle** : A line segment joining the vertex of a triangle to the mid point of the opposite side is known as the median of a triangle. A triangle has 3 medians.

AD is the median of △ ABC.

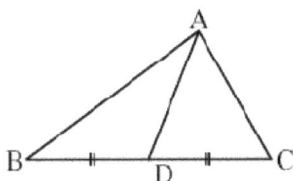

## Properties of Median

(i) Each median divides the triangle into two parts, and the areas of these two parts are equal.

In triangle ABC, the median AD divides the triangle into two parts: △ADC and △BDA.

Area of △ADC = Area of △BDA

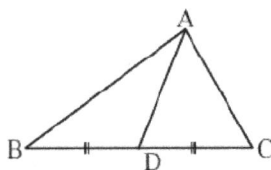

(ii) The three medians of a triangle are **concurrent.** i.e. they meet at a single point known as the **Centroid.** The medians AL, BM and CN meet at P, the centroid of the triangle.

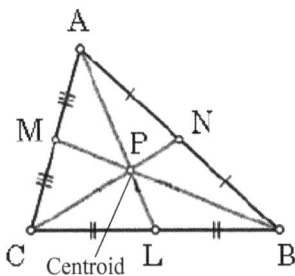

(iii) **Apollonius's Theorem** : The sum of the squares of any two sides of any triangle equals twice the square on half the third side, together with twice the square on the median bisecting the third side.

In any triangle ABC if AD is a median, then

$$AB^2 + AC^2 = 2(AD^2 + BD^2)$$

(iv) In △ABC if $a$, $b$ and $c$ are the sides of the triangle with respective medians $m_a$, $m_b$, and $m_c$ from their midpoints, then the lengths of the medians is given by:

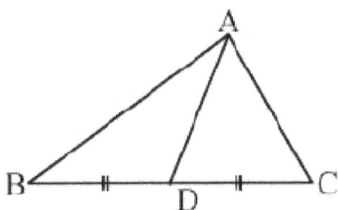

$$m_a = \sqrt{\frac{2b^2 + 2c^2 - a^2}{4}}$$

$$m_b = \sqrt{\frac{2a^2 + 2c^2 - b^2}{4}}$$

$$m_c = \sqrt{\frac{2a^2 + 2b^2 - c^2}{4}}$$

(v) Sum of the medians is less than the perimeter of the triangle.

$$m_a + m_b + m_c < AB + BC + CA$$

(vi) The medians from sides of lengths $a$ and $b$ are perpendicular if and only if:

$$a^2 + b^2 = 5c^2$$

(vii) Three times the sum of the square of the sides is equal to four times the sum of the square of the medians.

$$\frac{3}{4}(a^2 + b^2 + c^2) = m_a^2 + m_b^2 + m_c^2$$

(viii) The area of the triangle in terms of the median is given by:

$$\text{Area} = \frac{4}{3}\sqrt{s(s - m_a)(s - m_b)(s - m_c)}$$

$$\text{where } S = \frac{m_a + m_b + m_c}{2}$$

(ix) The centroid divides each median into two parts in the ratio 2:1, with the centroid being twice as close to the midpoint of a side as it is to the opposite vertex.

**Altitude of a triangle** : The perpendicular line segment from a vertex of a triangle to its opposite side is called an altitude of the triangle. A triangle has 3 altitudes.

PM is the altitude of ΔPQR.

## Properties of Altitude

(i) The point where all the altitudes of a triangle meet is known as the **orthocenter**. Altitudes AD, BE and CF meet at O the orthocenter of the triangle.

(ii) Orthocenter of a triangle is not always inside the triangle. It lies inside for an acute triangle, outside for an obtuse triangle and on the vertex of the right triangle.

# Orthocenter of Acute Triangle

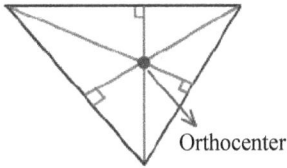

Orthocenter

# Orthocenter of Right Triangle

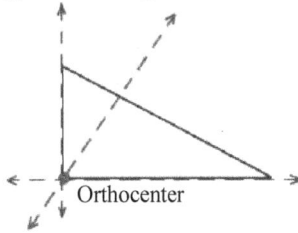

Orthocenter

# Orthocenter of Obtuse Triangle

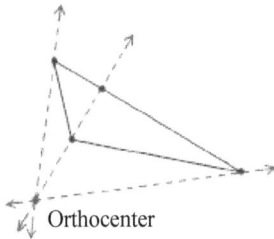

Orthocenter

# Perpendicular Bisector of a Triangle

A line segment that is both perpendicular and passes through the mid point of a side of a triangle is called the perpendicular bisector of the triangle. A triangle has 3 perpendicular bisectors. It may or may not join the opposite vertex.

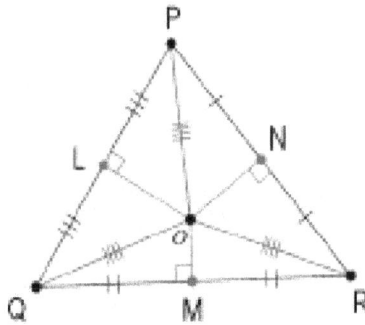

AD is the perpendicular bisector of ∆ABC. OM, ON and OL are the perpendicular bisectors of ∆PQR.

## Properties of Perpendicular Bisector

(i) The perpendicular bisectors of a triangle are concurrent. The point where three perpendicular bisectors of a triangle meet is known as the circumcenter.

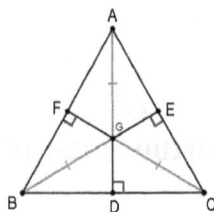

The perpendicular bisectors AD, BE and CF meet at a point G .

(ii) The circumcenter is equidistant from the vertices of the triangle i.e. GA = GB = GC

(iii) The circle that passes through all the three vertices of the triangle is known as circumcircle of a triangle. The circumcenter is the centre of the circumcircle.

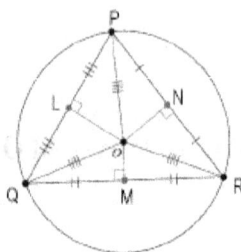

O is the centre of the circumcircle. OP, OQ and OR are the circumradius of the circumcircle.

a) Every triangle has a circumcircle.

b) The position of the circumcenter depends on the type of the triangle. It lies inside an acute triangle, outside an obtuse triangle and at the centre of the hypotenuse on a right triangle.

*Note:*

- In case of an equilateral triangle the centroid, incenter and circumcenter are coincident.
- Every perpendicular bisector is an altitude but every altitude is not a perpendicular bisector.
- Every perpendicular bisector is a median but every median is not a perpendicular bisector.

## Angle Bisector of a Triangle
### Definition

An angle bisector is a line segment or ray that divides an angle into two congruent angles.

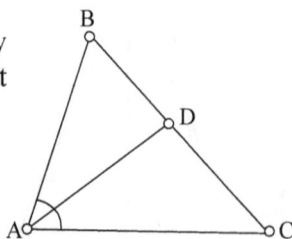

AD is the angle bisector of ∠ BAC i.e.

∠ BAD = ∠ DAC

## Properties of Angle Bisector of a Triangle

(i)  If a point lies on the bisector of an angle, then it is equidistant from the sides of the angle.

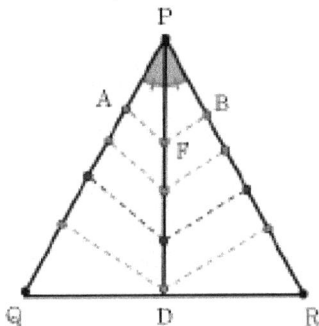

If PD is the angle bisector of $\angle$QPR, then AF = BF

(ii) *Angle Bisector Theorem* : This theorem states that the angle bisector of a triangle divides the sides of the triangle proportionally.

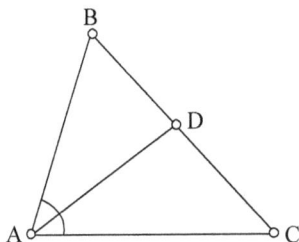

In $\triangle$ABC, if AD is the bisector of $\angle$BAC, then

$$\frac{BD}{DC} = \frac{AB}{AC}$$

(iii) The three angle bisectors of a triangle are concurrent. The point where the three angle bisectors of a triangle meet is called the incenter. The circle drawn with centre at incentre and radius equal to the perpendicular distance from incentre to any side of a triangle is known as incircle.

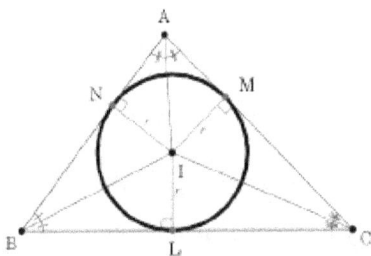

In $\triangle ABC$, AI, BI and CI are the angle bisectors, I is the incenter and IL, IM and IN are the inradius.

## CONGRUENCE OF TRIANGLES

Two triangles are congruent, if their corresponding sides are equal in length and their corresponding angles are equal in size. If triangle ABC is congruent to triangle DEF, the relationship can be written mathematically as:

$$\triangle ABC \cong \triangle DEF$$

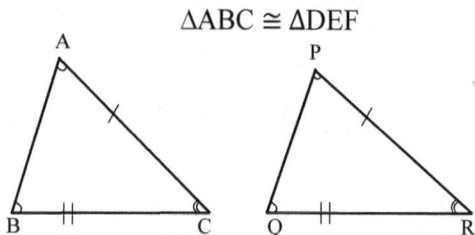

- Corresponding parts of congruent triangles are equal.
- In congruent triangles ABC and PQR, we have:

(i) Corresponding vertices: A and P, B and Q, C and R.

(ii) Corresponding sides: AB and PQ, BC and QR, AC and PR .

(iii) Corresponding angles: $\angle A$ and $\angle P$, $\angle B$ and $\angle Q$, $\angle C$ and $\angle R$.

## Properties of Congruence of Triangles
### Reflexive Property
Every triangle is congruent to itself.

### Symmetric Property
If $\triangle ABC \cong \triangle PQR$, then $\triangle PQR \cong \triangle ABC$

### Transitive Property
If $\triangle ABC \cong \triangle DEF$, $\triangle DEF \cong \triangle PQR$, then $\triangle ABC \cong \triangle PQR$.

## Congruency Rules
### Side Side Side (SSS)
If three sides of one triangle are equal to the corresponding three sides of the other triangle, then the two triangles are congruent.

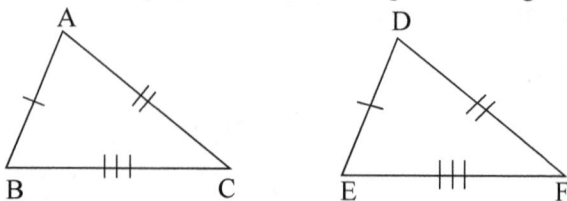

In $\triangle ABC$ and $\triangle DEF$, AB = DE, BC = EF and CA = FD, hence $\triangle ABC \cong \triangle DEF$ by SSS congruency rule.

## Side Angle Side (SAS)

If two sides and the included angle of one triangle are equal to two sides and the included angle of the other triangle, then the two triangles are congruent.

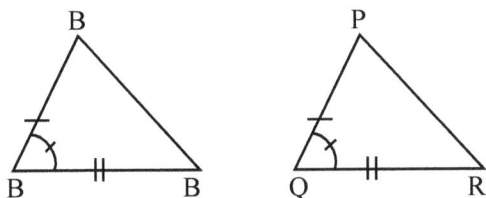

In ΔABC and ΔPQR, AB = QP, AC = QR and ∠BAC = ∠PQR, hence ΔABC ≅ ΔQPR by SAS congruency rule.

## Angle Side Angle (ASA)

If two angles and the included side of one triangle are equal to two angles and the included side of the other triangle, then the two triangles are congruent.

In ΔDEF and ΔPQR, EF = QR, ∠DEF = ∠PQR and
∠DFE = ∠PRQ, hence ΔDEF ≅ ΔPQR by ASA congruency rule.

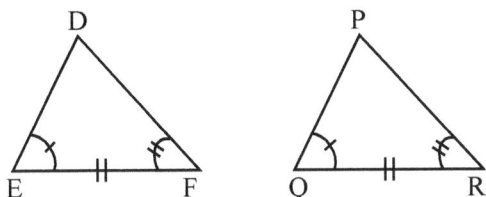

## Angle Angle Side (AAS)

If two angles and one side of one triangle are equal to two angles and the corresponding side of the other triangle, then the two triangles are congruent.

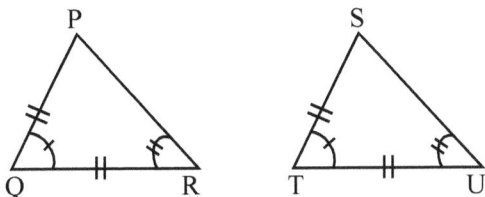

In ΔPQR and ΔSTU, PQ = ST, ∠PQR = ∠STU and
∠QRP = ∠TUS, hence ΔPQR ≅ ΔSTU by AAS congruency rule.

## RHS Rule

If in two right triangles, hypotenuse and one side of a triangle are equal to the hypotenuse and one side of other triangle, then the two triangles are congruent.

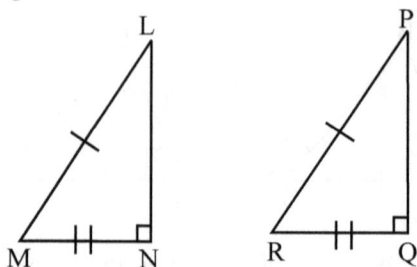

In $\triangle$LMN and $\triangle$PRQ, LM = PR, MN = RQ and

$\angle$LNM = $\angle$PQR = 90°, then $\triangle$LNM $\cong$ $\triangle$PQR by RHS congruency rule.

## Properties of a Triangle

(i) Exterior Angle Property

The measure of any exterior angle of a triangle is equal to the sum of the measures of its interior opposite angles.

$$\angle 1 + \angle 2 = \angle ACD$$

(ii) Angle Sum Property of a Triangle

The sum of the measure of three angles of a triangle is 180°.

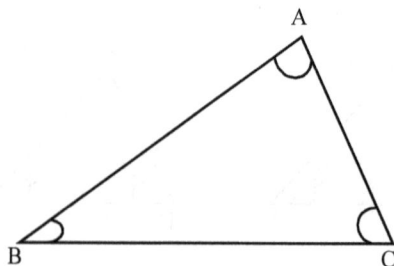

$$\angle A + \angle B + \angle C = 180°$$

(iii) Angles opposite to equal sides of a triangle are equal.

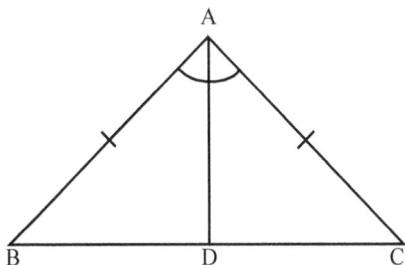

If AB = AC, ∠ACB = ∠ABC

(iv) Sides opposite to equal angles of a triangle are equal.

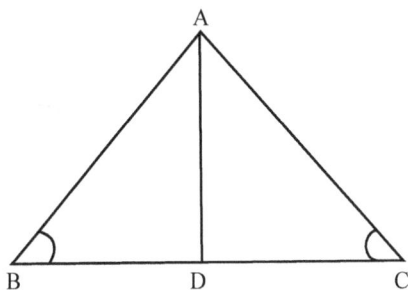

If ∠ACB = ∠ABC, then AB = AC

(v) Each angle of an equilateral triangle is of 60°.

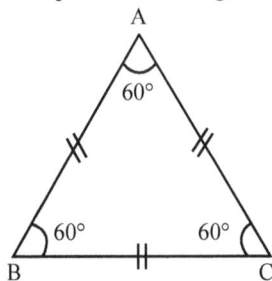

(vi) In a triangle, angle opposite to the longer side is larger (greater). In ΔABC, AC is the largest side, hence, ∠ABC is the largest angle.

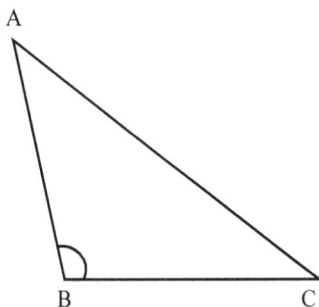

(vii) In a triangle, the side opposite to the larger (greater) angle is longer.

In $\triangle ABC$, $\angle ABC$ is the largest angle, hence AC is the largest side.

(viii) Sum of any two sides of a triangle is greater than the third side

$$AB + AC > BC$$
$$AB + BC > AC$$
$$BC + AC > AB$$

(ix) Two triangles on the same base (or equal bases) and between the same parallels are equal in area.

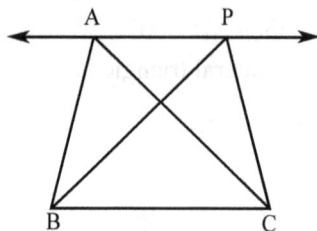

$\triangle ABC$ and $\triangle PBC$ lie on the same base BC and lie between the same parallels BC and AP hence, ar($\triangle ABC$) = ar($\triangle PBC$).

(x) Two triangles having equal areas and the same base (or equal bases) lie between the same parallels.

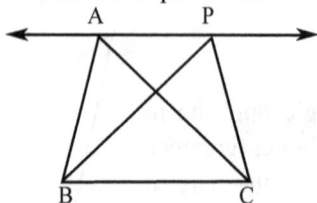

ar($\triangle ABC$) = ar($\triangle PBC$) and they lie on the same base BC, hence they lie between same parallels AP and BC.

## Mid Point Theorem

The line segment joining the mid-points of two sides of a triangle is parallel to the third side and half of it.

If E and F are the mid points of sides AB and AC respectively of a $\triangle ABC$ then

$$EF \parallel BC \text{ and } EF = \frac{1}{2}BC$$

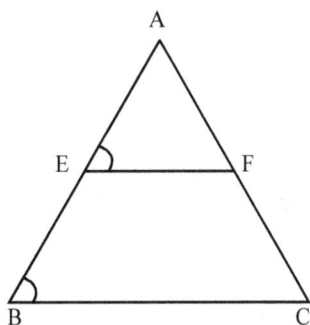

## Converse of Mid Point Theorem

The line drawn through the mid-point of one side of a triangle, parallel to another side bisects the third side.

If E is the mid point of side AB of $\triangle ABC$ and EF $\parallel$ BC, then F is the mid point of side AC.

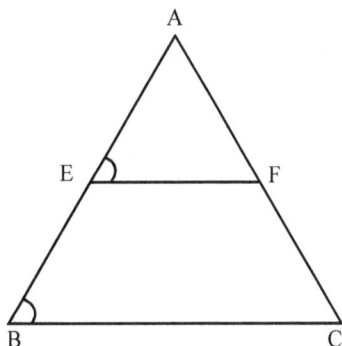

═══════ **SIMILARITY OF TRIANGLES** ═══════

## Definition

Two triangles are similar, if
  (i) their corresponding angles are equal and
  (ii) their corresponding sides are in the same ratio (or proportion).

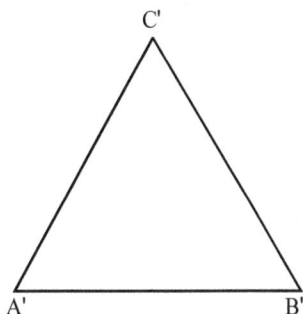

In $\triangle ABC$ and $\triangle A'B'C'$,

(i) $\angle A = \angle A'$, $\angle B = \angle B'$, $\angle C = \angle C'$

(ii) $\dfrac{AB}{A'B'} = \dfrac{BC}{B'C'} = \dfrac{CA}{C'A'}$

Hence, $\triangle ABC \sim \triangle A'B'C'$

*Note:* All congruent triangles are similar but all similar triangles are not congruent.

If corresponding angles of two triangles are equal, then they are known as **equiangular triangles**.

The ratio of any two corresponding sides in two equiangular triangles is always the same.

## Similarity Criterion

**AAA similarity** : If in two triangles, corresponding angles are equal, then their corresponding sides are in the same ratio and hence the two triangles are similar by AAA similarity criterion.

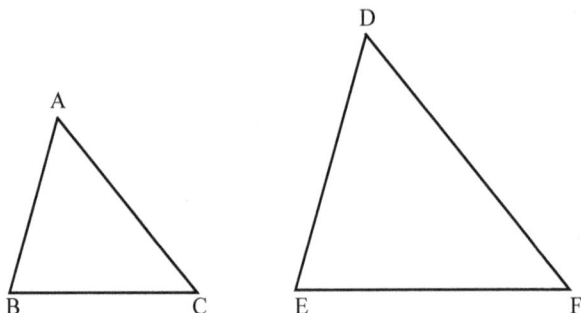

In $\triangle ABC$ and $\triangle DEF$,

if $\angle A = \angle D$, $\angle B = \angle E$ and $\angle C = \angle F$

then $\dfrac{AB}{DE} = \dfrac{BC}{EF} = \dfrac{CA}{DF}$

$\triangle ABC \sim \triangle DEF$ (AAA Similarity)

**AA similarity** : If in two triangles, two angles of one triangle are respectively equal to the two angles of the other triangle, then the two triangles are similar by AA similarity criterion.

If two angles of a triangle are respectively equal to two angles of another triangle, then by the angle sum property of a triangle their third angles will also be equal. Hence, AA similarity is same as AAA similarity.

**SSS similarity** : If in two triangles, corresponding sides are in the same ratio, then their corresponding angles are equal and hence the triangles are similar by SSS similarity criterion.

In $\triangle ABC$ and $\triangle DEF$,

if $\dfrac{AB}{DE}=\dfrac{BC}{EF}=\dfrac{AC}{DF}$

then $\angle A=\angle D$, $\angle B=\angle E$ and $\angle C=\angle F$

$\triangle ABC \sim \triangle DEF$ (SSS Similarity)

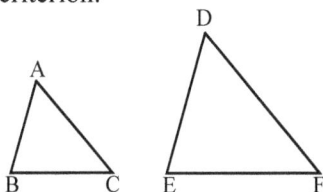

**SAS similarity** : If one angle of a triangle is equal to one angle of another triangle and the sides including these angles are in the same ratio (proportional), then the triangles are similar by SAS similarity criterion.

In $\triangle ABC$ and $\triangle DEF$,

if $\dfrac{AB}{DE}=\dfrac{AC}{DF}$ (<1) and $\angle A=\angle D$ then

$\triangle ABC \sim \triangle DEF$ (SAS Similarity)

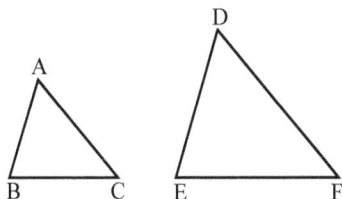

## Properties of Similar Triangle

(i) **Basic Proportionality Theorem (Thales Theorem)** : If a line is drawn parallel to one side of a triangle to intersect the other two sides at distinct points, then the other two sides are divided in the same ratio.

In $\triangle ABC$, DE is parallel to BC and intersects AB at D and AC at E then

$$\dfrac{AD}{DB}=\dfrac{AE}{EC}$$

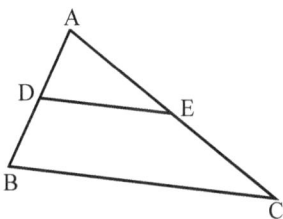

(ii) If a line divides any two sides of a triangle in the same ratio, then the line is parallel to the third side.

In $\triangle ABC$ if $\dfrac{AD}{DB}=\dfrac{AE}{EC}$

then DE $\parallel$ BC

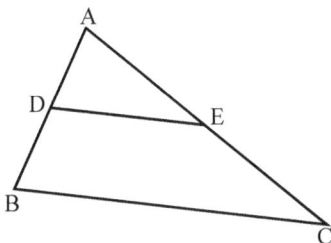

(iii) The ratio of the areas of two similar triangles is equal to the square of the ratio of their corresponding sides.

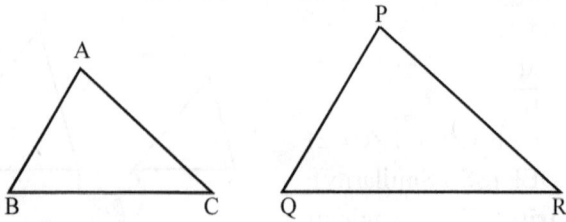

If $\triangle ABC \sim \triangle PQR$

then $\dfrac{ar(ABC)}{ar(PQR)} = \left(\dfrac{AB}{PQ}\right)^2 = \left(\dfrac{BC}{QR}\right)^2 = \left(\dfrac{CA}{RP}\right)^2$

(iv) Perimeters of similar triangles are in the same ratio as the scale factor (When two triangles are similar, the reduced ratio of any two corresponding sides is called the scale factor of the similar triangles).

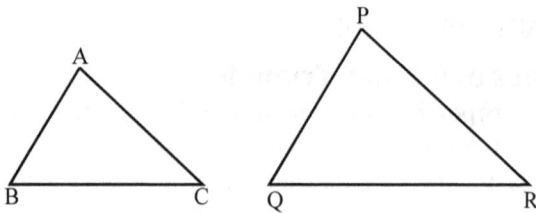

If $\triangle ABC \sim \triangle PQR$, then

$$\dfrac{\text{Perimeters of } \triangle ABC}{\text{Perimeters of } \triangle PQR} = \dfrac{\text{Length of AB}}{\text{Length of PQ}} = \dfrac{\text{Length of BC}}{\text{Length of QR}} = \dfrac{\text{Length of CA}}{\text{Length of RP}}$$

(v) If a perpendicular is drawn from the vertex of the right angle of a right triangle to the hypotenuse, then the triangles on both sides of the perpendicular are similar to the whole triangle and also to each other.

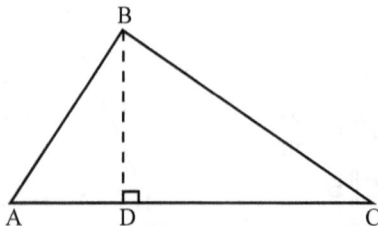

In right angled triangle ABC right angled at B, a perpendicular BD is drawn on the hypotenuse AC, then

$$\Delta ADB \sim \Delta ABC, \Delta BDC \sim \Delta ABC, \text{ and } \Delta ADB \sim \Delta BDC$$

## QUADRILATERAL

A quadrilateral is a polygon with four sides and four vertices.

| Quadrilateral | Properties |
|---|---|
| Square | • A square is a regular quadrilateral.<br>• All angles are equal (90°).<br>• All sides are of equal length.<br>• Opposite sides are parallel<br>• The diagonals bisect each other at 90°<br>• The diagonals are equal in length. |
| Rhombus | • Diagonally opposite angles are equal.<br>• All sides are of equal lengths.<br>• Opposite sides are parallel<br>• The diagonals bisect each other at 90° |
| Rectangle | • All angles are equal (90°)<br>• Opposite sides are of equal length.<br>• The diagonals are equal in length |
| Parallelogram | • Diagonally opposite angles are equal.<br>• Opposite sides are of equal length<br>• Opposite sides are parallel<br>• The diagonals bisect each other. |
| Trapezium | • One pair of opposite sides is parallel |
| Kite | • Two pairs of sides are of equal length<br>• One pair of diagonally opposite angles is equal.<br>• Only one diagonal is bisected by the other.<br>• The diagonals cross at 90° |

*Note:*

Every rectangle is a parallelogram but not vice versa.

Every square is a rhombus but not vice versa.

**Some other Properties**

* The sum of four interior angles of a quadrilateral is 360°.
* The quadrilateral formed by joining the mid-points of the sides of a quadrilateral, in order, is a parallelogram.

# Condition for Quadrilateral to be a Parallelogram

A quadrilateral is a parallelogram, if

(i) opposite sides are equal or

(ii) opposite angles are equal or

(iii) a pair of opposite sides is equal and parallel or

(iv) diagonals bisect each other

# Property of a Parallelogram

(i) Parallelograms on the same base and between the same parallels are equal in area.

Parallelograms PQRS and PQTU are on the same base PQ and between same parallels PQ and UR, hence

$$ar(PQRS) = ar(PQTU)$$

(ii) Parallelograms on the same base (or equal bases) and having equal areas lie between the same parallels.

Parallelograms PQRS and PQTU are on the same base PQ and if ar(PQRS) = ar(PQTU), then the parallelograms lie between the same parallels PQ and UR.

## Triangle and Parallelogram on the Same Base

If a triangle and a parallelogram are on the same base and between the same parallels, the area of the triangle is equal to half the area of the parallelogram.

$\triangle$ABP and parallelogram ABCD lie on the same base AB and between same parallels AB and PC then

$$\text{ar}(\triangle ABC) = \frac{1}{2}\text{ar}(ABCD)$$

## ══ CIRCLE ══

### Definition

A circle is the collection of all points in a plane, which are equidistant from a fixed point in the plane. The fixed point is known as the **centre** of the circle and the fixed distance is called the **radius**.

A line segment whose end points lie on the circle is known as a **chord**.

A chord which passes through the centre of the circle is known as a **diameter**. Diameter = 2 × Radius

*Note:*

Diameter is the longest chord of a circle.

Every diameter is a chord but every chord is not a diameter.

### Circle and its Related Terms

**Circular Region :** A circle divides the plane on which it lies into three parts.

(i) Interior of the circle (inside portion of the circle)
(ii) The circle
(iii) Exterior of the circle (outside portion of the circle)

The circle along with its interior is called the circular region.

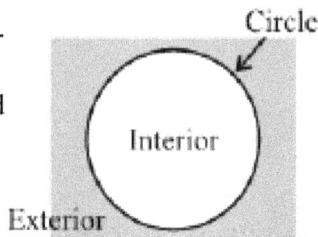

**Circumference :** The linear distance around the edge of a circle is known as circumference.

**Arc :** Any part of the circumference of a circle is known as an arc.

**Major and Minor Arc :** The larger arc joining two points on the circumference of a circle is known as a major arc. The shorter arc joining two points on the circumference of a circle is known as a minor arc.

**Segment of a Circle :** The region between a chord and a major or minor arc is called a segment of a circle. The region between a chord and a major arc is called a *major segment* of a circle. The region between a chord and a *minor arc* is called a minor segment of a circle.

**Sector :** The region between two radii and the arc joining the end points of the radii is known as a sector. The region between two radii and the minor arc is known as *minor sector*. The region between two radii and the major arc is known as *major sector*.

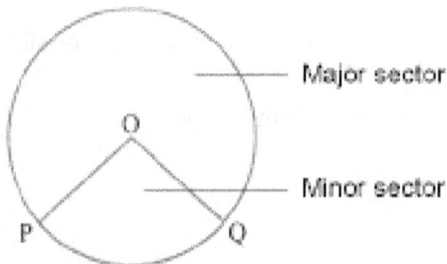

**Semi Circle :** Half of a circle is known as a semi circle.

In a semi circle, the major arc is equal to the minor arc, the major segment is equal to the minor segment and the major sector is equal to the minor sector.

## Cyclic Quadrilateral

A quadrilateral ABCD is said to be cyclic if all the four vertices A, B, C and D lie on the circle.

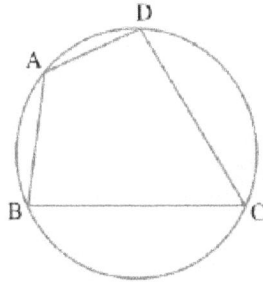

## Tangent of a Circle

A line that intersects the circle at only one point is known as the tangent of a circle.

- The common point of the tangent and the circle is called the point of contact and the tangent is said to touch the circle at the point of contact.
- There is only one tangent at a point of the circle.
- The line containing the radius through the point of contact is called the normal to the circle at the point.

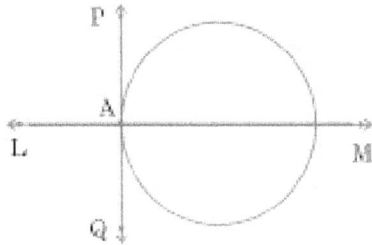

Line PQ is the tangent of the circle. Point A is the point of contact. Line LM is the normal.

## Length of Tangent

Length of the tangent from an external point is the length of the segment between the external point and the point of contact.

PQ and PR are the length of the tangents from an external point P of the circle.

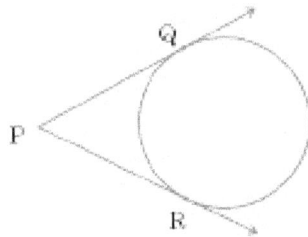

## Secant of a Circle

A line that intersects the circle at two points is known as the secant of a circle.

- ◆ The tangent to a circle is a special case of the secant, when the two end points of its corresponding chord coincide.

Line PQ is the secant of the circle.

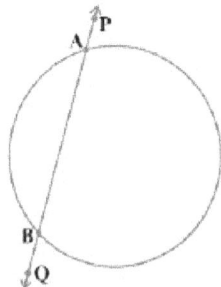

## Properties of a Circle

(i) Equal chords of a circle (or of congruent circles) subtend equal angles at the centre.

If chord AB is equal to chord CD of a circle with centre O, then $\angle AOB = \angle COD$

(ii) If the angles subtended by two chords of a circle (or of congruent circles) at the centre (corresponding centres) are equal, the chords are equal.

If $\angle AOB = \angle COD$ in a circle with centre O, then chord AB = chord CD.

(iii) The perpendicular from the centre of a circle to a chord bisects the chord.

If $\angle OMA = \angle OMB = 90°$ in a circle with centre O and chord AB, then AM = MB.

(iv) The line drawn through the centre of a circle to bisect a chord is perpendicular to the chord.

If OM is drawn in such a way that AM = MB, then $\angle OMB = 90°$

(v) There is one and only one circle passing through three non-collinear points.

There is only one circle passing through three non collinear points A, B and C.

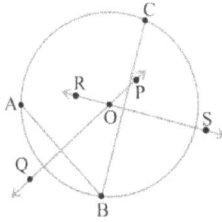

(vi) Equal chords of a circle (or of congruent circles) are equidistant from the centre (or corresponding centres).

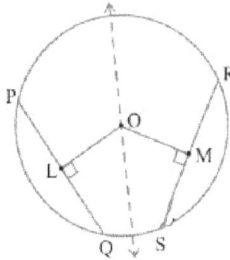

If chord PQ is equal to chord RS, then the perpendicular distance from the centre, OL = OM.

(vii) Chords equidistant from the centre (or corresponding centres) of a circle (or of congruent circles) are equal.

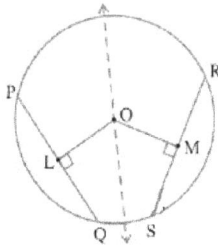

If the perpendicular distance from the centre OL = OM, then the chord PQ = chord RS.

(viii) If two arcs of a circle are congruent, then their corresponding chords are equal and conversely. If two chords of a circle are equal, then their corresponding arcs (minor, major) are congruent.

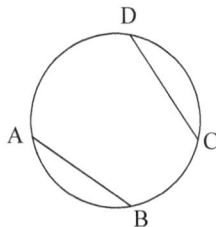

If chord AB = chord DC, then arc AB = arc DC and if arc AB = arc DC, then chord AB = chord DC.

(ix)  Congruent arcs of a circle subtend equal angles at the centre.

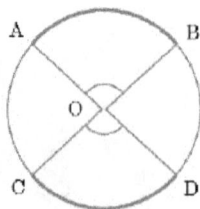

If arc AB = arc CD, then ∠AOB = ∠COD

(x)   The angle subtended by an arc at the centre is double the angle subtended by it at any point on the remaining part of the circle.

If arc PQ of the circle subtends an angle POQ at the centre and PAQ at a point on the remaining part of the circle, then

$$\angle POQ = 2\angle PAQ$$

(xi)  Angles in the same segment of a circle are equal.

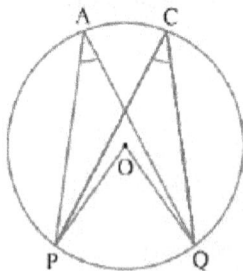

If two angles PCQ and PAQ are formed in the same segment, then

$$\angle PCQ = \angle PAQ$$

(xii) Angle in a semicircle is a right angle. If arc PAQ forms a semi circle, then

$$\angle PAQ = 90°$$

Maths Formulae For School Students

(xiii) If a line segment joining two points subtends equal angles at two other points lying on the same side of the line containing the line segment, the four points lie on a circle.

If a line segment AB subtends two equal angles ACB and ADB and if E and E' lie on the same side of AB as C and D, then E and E' coincide with D.

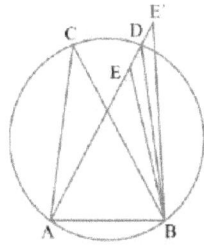

(xiv) The sum of either pair of opposite angles of a cyclic quadrilateral is $180^0$. If ABCD is a cyclic quadrilateral, then $\angle A + \angle C = \angle B + \angle D = 180°$

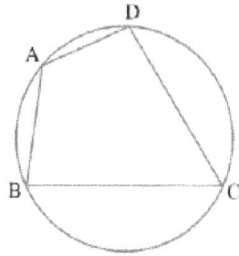

(xv) If sum of a pair of opposite angles of a quadrilateral is $180^0$, the quadrilateral is cyclic.

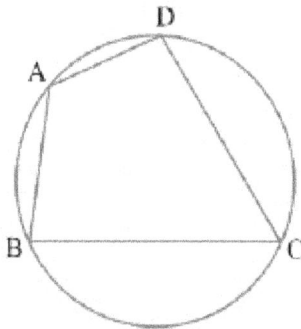

If $\angle A + \angle C = \angle B + \angle D = 180°$, then quadrilateral ABCD is a cyclic quadrilateral.

## Properties of a Tangent

(i) The tangent to a circle is perpendicular to the radius through the point of contact.

If XY is a tangent to the circle with point of contact P, then the radius OP is perpendicular to the tangent at P.

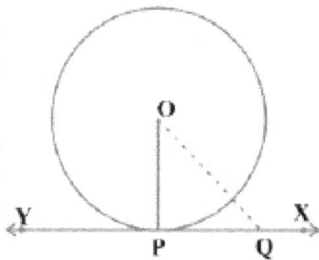

(ii) The lengths of the two tangents from an external point to a circle are equal.

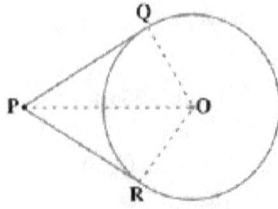

If a point P lies outside a circle with centre O and two tangents PQ and PR are drawn, then PQ = PR.

## POLYGON

# Types of Polygon

(i) **Regular Polygon**: A regular polygon has sides of equal length and all its interior angles are of equal measure. Regular polygons are both equiangular and equilateral.

(ii) **Irregular Polygon**: Irregular polygons can have sides of any length and angles of any measure.

Polygons of all types can be regular or irregular.

| Name | Regular | Irregular |
|---|---|---|
| Triangle | | |
| Quadrilateral | | |
| Pentagon | | |
| Hexagon | | |
| Octagon | | |

(iii) **Equiangular Polygon** : In this polygon, all angles are equal.

Rectangle

(iv) **Equilateral Polygon** : In this polygon, all sides are equal.

Rhombus

(v) **Convex Polygon** : A polygon with all its interior angles less than or equal to 180° is known as a convex polygon. In a convex polygon, every line segment between two vertices remains inside or on the boundary of the polygon. The Regular polygons are always convex.

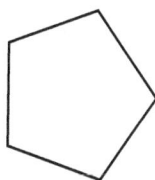

Regular Pentagon

(vi) **Concave Polygon** : A polygon with one or more interior angles greater than 180° is known as a concave polygon.

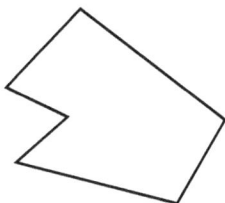

(vii) **Crossed Polygon** : A polygon where one or more sides crossed back over itself is called a crossed polygon. Most of the properties and theorems concerning polygons do not apply to this shape.

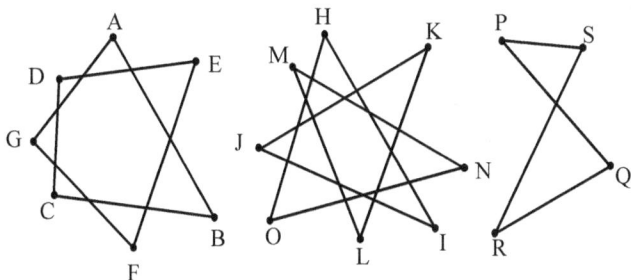

## Similarity of Polygons

Two polygons of the same number of sides are similar, if

(i) their corresponding angles are equal and

(ii) their corresponding sides are in the same ratio (or proportion).

# Properties of Polygons (Regular and Irregular)

(i) **Interior angles** : For a regular polygon all the interior angles are the same. For an irregular polygon, each angle may be different.

Interion angle

Exterior angle

a) The sum of the interior angles of a simple $n$-gon is $(n-2)\,\pi$ radians

or $(n-2)\,180°$, where $n$ is the number of sides in a polygon.

b) Each interior angle is given by
$$\frac{(n-2)180°}{n}$$

(ii) a) The sum of the measures of the exterior angles of a polygon, one at each vertex is $360°$.

b) Each angle of a regular convex polygon of $n$ sides is $\dfrac{360}{n}$

3. **Diagonals** : The diagonals of a polygon are lines joining any two non-adjacent vertices. A diagonal may lie outside the polygon as well.

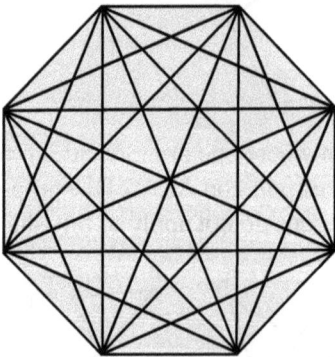

An octagon has
20 diagonals

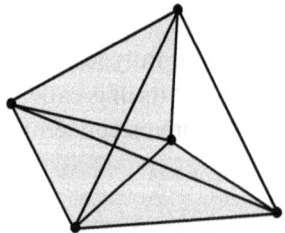

The number of diagonals of a $n$ sided polygon is given by $\dfrac{n(n-3)}{2}$

# ④

## Trigonometry Formulae

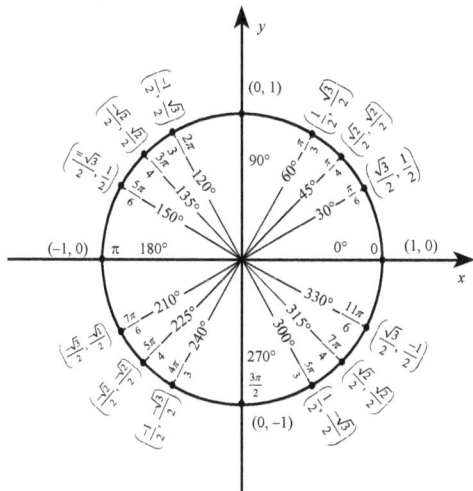

Cosine and Sine Around the Unit Circle

## Pythagoras Theorem

In a right triangle, the square of the hypotenuse (the side opposite to the right angle) is equal to the sum of the square of the other two sides.

**Converse of Pythagoras Theorem :** If in a triangle, square of one side is equal to the sum of the squares of the other two sides, then the angle opposite the first side is a right angle.

$$a^2 + b^2 = c^2$$

In $\triangle ABC$ if $c^2 = a^2 + b^2$, then the angle opposite to side c i.e angle C is a right angle.

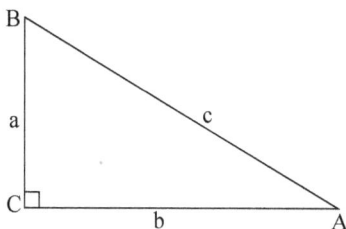

*Pythagorean Triplet*

For any natural number $n > 1$, $(2n)^2 + (n^2 - 1)^2 = (n^2 + 1)^2$. Hence $2n$, $n^2 - 1$ and $n^2 + 1$ form a Pythagorean triplet.

## Trigonometric Ratio Definition

Trigonometric ratio is a ratio that describes a relationship between a side and angle of a right triangle.

## Trigonometric Ratios in Right Triangles

There are six trigonometric ratios in right triangles.

$$\sin\theta = \frac{\text{length of opposite side}}{\text{length of hypotenuse}}$$

$$\cos\theta = \frac{\text{length of adjacent side}}{\text{length of hypotenuse}}$$

$$\tan\theta = \frac{\text{length of opposite side}}{\text{length of adjacent side}}$$

$$\sec\theta = \frac{\text{length of hypotenuse}}{\text{length of adjacent side}}$$

$$\text{cosec}\,\theta = \frac{\text{length of hypotenuse}}{\text{length of opposite side}}$$

$$\cot\theta = \frac{\text{length of adjacent side}}{\text{length of opposite side}}$$

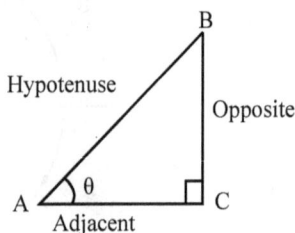

## Relation Between Various Trigonometric Ratios

$$\tan\theta = \frac{\sin\theta}{\cos\theta}, \quad \sec\theta = \frac{1}{\cos\theta}$$

$$\text{cosec}\,\theta = \frac{1}{\sin\theta}, \quad \cot\theta = \frac{1}{\tan\theta} = \frac{\cos\theta}{\sin\theta}$$

Maths Formulae For School Students

| In terms of | $\sin\theta$ | $\cos\theta$ | $\tan\theta$ | $\csc\theta$ | $\sec\theta$ | $\cot\theta$ |
|---|---|---|---|---|---|---|
| $\sin\theta =$ | $\sin\theta$ | $\pm\sqrt{1-\cos^2\theta}$ | $\pm\dfrac{\tan\theta}{\sqrt{1+\tan^2\theta}}$ | $\dfrac{1}{\csc\theta}$ | $\pm\dfrac{\sqrt{\sec^2\theta-1}}{\sec\theta}$ | $\pm\dfrac{1}{\sqrt{1+\cot^2\theta}}$ |
| $\cos\theta =$ | $\pm\sqrt{1-\sin^2\theta}$ | $\cos\theta$ | $\pm\dfrac{1}{\sqrt{1+\tan^2\theta}}$ | $\pm\dfrac{\sqrt{\csc^2\theta-1}}{\csc\theta}$ | $\dfrac{1}{\sec\theta}$ | $\pm\dfrac{\cot\theta}{\sqrt{1+\cot^2\theta}}$ |
| $\tan\theta =$ | $\pm\dfrac{\sin\theta}{\sqrt{1-\sin^2\theta}}$ | $\pm\dfrac{\sqrt{1-\cos^2\theta}}{\cos\theta}$ | $\tan\theta$ | $\pm\dfrac{1}{\sqrt{\csc^2\theta-1}}$ | $\pm\sqrt{\sec^2\theta-1}$ | $\dfrac{1}{\cot\theta}$ |
| $\csc\theta =$ | $\dfrac{1}{\sin\theta}$ | $\pm\dfrac{1}{\sqrt{1-\cos^2\theta}}$ | $\pm\dfrac{\sqrt{1+\tan^2\theta}}{\tan\theta}$ | $\csc\theta$ | $\pm\dfrac{\sec\theta}{\sqrt{\sec^2\theta-1}}$ | $\pm\sqrt{1+\cot^2\theta}$ |
| $\sec\theta =$ | $\pm\dfrac{1}{\sqrt{1-\sin^2\theta}}$ | $\dfrac{1}{\cos\theta}$ | $\pm\sqrt{1+\tan^2\theta}$ | $\pm\dfrac{\csc\theta}{\sqrt{\csc^2\theta-1}}$ | $\sec\theta$ | $\pm\dfrac{\sqrt{1+\cot^2\theta}}{\cot\theta}$ |
| $\cot\theta =$ | $\pm\dfrac{\sqrt{1-\sin^2\theta}}{\sin\theta}$ | $\pm\dfrac{\cos\theta}{\sqrt{1-\cos^2\theta}}$ | $\dfrac{1}{\tan\theta}$ | $\pm\sqrt{\csc^2\theta-1}$ | $\pm\dfrac{1}{\sqrt{\sec^2\theta-1}}$ | $\cot\theta$ |

Each trigonometric function in terms of the other five

*Note:* The values of the trigonometric ratios of an angle do not vary with the lengths of the sides of the triangle, if the angle remains the same.

## Trigonometric Table

1 full circle = 360 degrees = $2\pi$ radians

| $\theta$ (Radian) | 0 | $\dfrac{\pi}{6}$ | $\dfrac{\pi}{4}$ | $\dfrac{\pi}{3}$ | $\dfrac{\pi}{2}$ |
|---|---|---|---|---|---|
| $\theta$ (Degree) | 0° | 30° | 45° | 60° | 90° |
| $\sin\theta$ | 0 | $\dfrac{1}{2}$ | $\dfrac{1}{\sqrt{2}}$ | $\dfrac{\sqrt{3}}{2}$ | 1 |
| $\cos\theta$ | 1 | $\dfrac{\sqrt{3}}{2}$ | $\dfrac{1}{\sqrt{2}}$ | $\dfrac{1}{2}$ | 0 |
| $\tan\theta$ | 0 | $\dfrac{1}{\sqrt{3}}$ | 1 | $\sqrt{3}$ | Not defined |
| $\cot\theta$ | Not defined | $\sqrt{3}$ | 1 | $\dfrac{1}{\sqrt{3}}$ | 0 |
| $\sec\theta$ | 1 | $\dfrac{2}{\sqrt{3}}$ | $\sqrt{2}$ | 2 | Not defined |
| $\operatorname{cosec}\theta$ | Not defined | 2 | $\sqrt{2}$ | $\dfrac{2}{\sqrt{3}}$ | 1 |

## Pythagorean Identity

$\sin^2\theta + \cos^2\theta = 1$, where $0° \leq \theta \leq 90°$

$1 + \tan^2\theta = \sec^2\theta$, where $0° \leq \theta < 90°$

$1 + \cot^2\theta = \csc^2\theta$, where $0° < \theta \leq 90°$

## Symmetry in Trigonometric Functions

$\sin(-\theta) = -\sin\theta$

$\cos(-\theta) = +\cos\theta$

$\tan(-\theta) = -\tan\theta$

$\csc(-\theta) = -\csc\theta$

$\sec(-\theta) = +\sec\theta$

$\cot(-\theta) = -\cot\theta$

## Trigonometric Ratios of Complementary Angles

$\sin(\frac{\pi}{2} - \theta) = +\cos\theta$

$\cos(\frac{\pi}{2} - \theta) = +\sin\theta$

$\tan(\frac{\pi}{2} - \theta) = +\cot\theta$

$\csc(\frac{\pi}{2} - \theta) = +\sec\theta$

$\sec(\frac{\pi}{2} - \theta) = +\csc\theta$

$\cot(\frac{\pi}{2} - \theta) = +\tan\theta$

## PERIODICITY IN TRIGONOMETRIC FUNCTIONS

$\sin(\theta + \frac{\pi}{2}) = +\cos\theta$

$\cos(\theta + \frac{\pi}{2}) = -\sin\theta$

$\tan(\theta + \frac{\pi}{2}) = -\cot\theta$

$\csc(\theta + \frac{\pi}{2}) = +\sec\theta$

$\sec(\theta + \frac{\pi}{2}) = -\csc\theta$

$\cot(\theta + \frac{\pi}{2}) = -\tan\theta$

$\sin(\theta + \pi) = -\sin\theta$

$\cos(\theta + \pi) = -\cos\theta$

$\tan(\theta + \pi) = +\tan\theta$

$\csc(\theta + \pi) = -\csc\theta$

$\sec(\theta + \pi) = -\sec\theta$

$\cot(\theta + \pi) = +\cot\theta$

$\sin(\pi - \theta) = +\sin\theta$

$\cos(\pi - \theta) = -\cos\theta$

$\tan(\pi - \theta) = -\tan\theta$

$\csc(\pi - \theta) = +\csc\theta$

$\sec(\pi - \theta) = -\sec\theta$

$\cot(\pi - \theta) = -\cot\theta$

$\sin(\theta + 2\pi) = +\sin\theta$

$\cos(\theta + 2\pi) = +\cos\theta$

$\tan(\theta + 2\pi) = +\tan\theta$

$\csc(\theta + 2\pi) = +\csc\theta$

$\sec(\theta + 2\pi) = +\sec\theta$

$\cot(\theta + 2\pi) = +\cot\theta$

$\sin(2\pi - \theta) = -\sin\theta$

$\cos(2\pi - \theta) = +\cos\theta$

$\tan(2\pi - \theta) = -\tan\theta$

$\csc(2\pi - \theta) = -\csc\theta$

$\sec(2\pi - \theta) = +\sec\theta$

$\cot(2\pi - \theta) = -\cot\theta$

## Trigonometric Equations

$\sin\theta = 0$ implies $\theta = n\pi$, where $n$ is any integer

$\cos\theta = 0$ implies $\theta = (2n + 1)\frac{\pi}{2}$ where $n$ is any integer

$\sin x = \sin y$ implies $x = n\pi + (-1)^n y$, where $n \in Z$

$\cos x = \cos y$ implies $x = 2n\pi \pm y$, where $n \in Z$

$\tan x = \tan y$ implies $x = n\pi + y$, where $n \in Z$

## Signs of Trigonometric Functions in Different Quadrants

|  | I | II | III | IV |
|---|---|---|---|---|
| Sinθ | + | + | − | − |
| Cosθ | + | − | − | + |
| Tanθ | + | − | + | − |
| Cosecθ | + | + | − | − |
| Secθ | + | − | − | + |
| Cotθ | + | − | + | − |

## Domain and Range of Trigonometric Functions

| Trigono-metric Function | Domain | Range |
|---|---|---|
| $y = \sin x$ | {Real numbers} | $[-1,1]$ |
| $y = \cos x$ | {Real numbers} | $[-1,1]$ |
| $y = \tan x$ | $\{x : x \in R \text{ and } x \neq (2n+1)\,\dfrac{\pi}{2}, n \in Z\}$ | {Real numbers} |
| $y = \operatorname{cosec} x$ | $\{x : x \in R \text{ and } x \neq n\pi, n \in Z\}$ | $\{y:y \in R, y \geq 1$ or $y \leq -1\}$ |
| $y = \sec x$ | $\{x : x \in R \text{ and } x \neq (2n+1)\,\dfrac{\pi}{2}, n \in Z\}$ | $\{y:y \in R, y \geq 1$ or $y \leq -1\}$ |
| $y = \cot x$ | $\{x : x \in R \text{ and } x \neq n\pi, n \in Z\}$ | {Real numbers} |

## Area of Triangle

If $a$, $b$, $c$ are the lengths of sides of a triangle and A, B, C are the opposite angles, then

Area of $\triangle ABC = \dfrac{1}{2}ab \sin C$

Or

Area of $\triangle ABC = \dfrac{1}{2}bc \sin A$

Or

Area of $\triangle ABC = \dfrac{1}{2}ac \sin B$

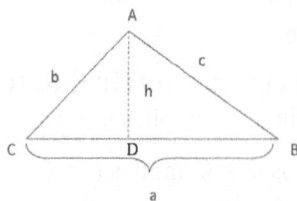

## Law of Sine

If *a, b, c* are the lengths of sides of a triangle; A, B, C are the opposite angles and D is the diameter of the circumcircle of the triangle, then

$$\frac{a}{\sin A} = \frac{b}{\sin B} = \frac{c}{\sin C} = D$$

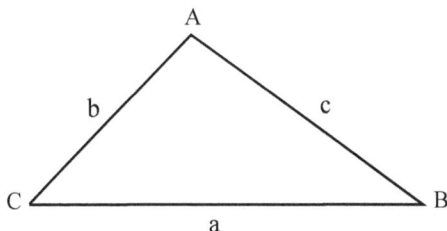

## Law of Cosine

If *a, b, c* are the lengths of sides of a triangle; A, B, C are the opposite angles, then

$$c^2 = a^2 + b^2 - 2ab \cos C$$
$$a^2 = b^2 + c^2 - 2bc \cos A$$
$$b^2 = a^2 + c^2 - 2ac \cos B$$

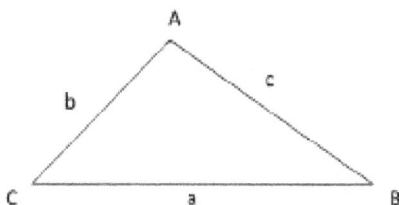

## Double Angle

$$\sin(2A) = 2\sin(A)\cos(A)$$
$$\sin(2A) = \frac{2\tan(A)}{1+\tan^2(A)}$$
$$\cos(2A) = 1 - 2\sin^2(A)$$
$$\cos(2A) = 2\cos^2(A) - 1$$
$$\cos(2A) = \cos^2(A) - \sin^2(A)$$
$$\cos(2A) = \frac{1-\tan^2(A)}{1+\tan^2(A)}$$
$$\tan(2A) = \frac{2\tan(A)}{1-\tan^2(A)}$$

## Half Angle

$$\sin\left(\frac{A}{2}\right) = \pm\sqrt{\frac{1-\cos(A)}{2}}$$

$$\cos\left(\frac{A}{2}\right) = \pm\sqrt{\frac{1+\cos(A)}{2}}$$

$$\tan\left(\frac{A}{2}\right) = \pm\frac{1-\cos(A)}{\sin(A)}$$

## Triple Angle

$$\sin(3A) = 3\sin(A) - 4\sin^3(A)$$

$$\cos(3A) = 4\cos^3(A) - 3\cos(A)$$

$$\tan(3A) = \frac{3\tan(A) - \tan^3(A)}{1 - 3\tan^2(A)}$$

## Sum to Product

$$\sin(A) + \sin(B) = 2\sin\left(\frac{A+B}{2}\right)\cos\left(\frac{A-B}{2}\right)$$

$$\sin(A) - \sin(B) = 2\cos\left(\frac{A+B}{2}\right)\sin\left(\frac{A-B}{2}\right)$$

$$\cos(A) + \cos(B) = 2\cos\left(\frac{A+B}{2}\right)\cos\left(\frac{A-B}{2}\right)$$

$$\cos(A) - \cos(B) = -2\sin\left(\frac{A+B}{2}\right)\sin\left(\frac{A-B}{2}\right)$$

## Product to Sum

$$2\cos(A)\cos(B) = \cos(A+B) + \cos(A-B)$$

$$-2\sin(A)\sin(B) = \cos(A+B) - \cos(A-B)$$

$$2\sin(A)\cos(B) = \sin(A+B) + \sin(A-B)$$

$$2\cos(A)\sin(B) = \sin(A+B) - \sin(A-B)$$

## Sum and Difference

$$\sin(A+B) = \sin(A)\cos(B) + \cos(A)\sin(B)$$

$$\sin(A-B) = \sin(A)\cos(B) - \cos(A)\sin(B)$$

$$\cos(A+B) = \cos(A)\cos(B) - \sin(A)\sin(B)$$

$$\cos(A-B) = \cos(A)\cos(B) + \sin(A)\sin(B)$$

$$\tan(A+B) = \frac{\tan(A) + \tan(B)}{1 - \tan(A)\tan(B)}$$

$$\tan(A-B) = \frac{\tan(A) - \tan(B)}{1 + \tan(A)\tan(B)}$$

$$\cot(A+B) = \frac{\cot(A)\cot(B)-1}{\cot(B)+\cot(A)}$$

$$\cot(A-B) = \frac{\cot(A)\cot(B)+1}{\cot(B)-\cot(A)}$$

## Sum of Sine and Cosine

$a_1\sin(Bt) + a_2\cos(Bt) = a\sin(Bt + \phi)$

where $a = \sqrt{a_1 + a_2}$ and $\tan(\phi) = \dfrac{a_2}{a_1}$

$\phi$ satisfies $\cos(\phi) = \dfrac{a_1}{a}$ and $\sin(\phi) = \dfrac{a_2}{a}$

## Euler's Formula

$e^{ix} = \cos x + i\sin x$, where $i = \sqrt{-1}$

$e^{i\pi} + 1 = 0$

## Inverse Trigonometric Functions

The domain and range (principal value branch) of inverse trigonometric functions are given by:

| Functions | Domain | Range (Principal Value Branch) |
|---|---|---|
| $y = \sin^{-1}x$ | $[-1, 1]$ | $\left[\dfrac{-\pi}{2}, \dfrac{\pi}{2}\right]$ |
| $y = \cos^{-1}x$ | $[-1, 1]$ | $[0, \pi]$ |
| $y = \operatorname{cosec}^{-1}x$ | $R-(-1, 1)$ | $\left[\dfrac{-\pi}{2}, \dfrac{\pi}{2}\right] - \{0\}$ |
| $y = \sec^{-1}x$ | $R-(-1, 1)$ | $[0, \pi] - \left\{\dfrac{\pi}{2}\right\}$ |
| $y = \tan^{-1}x$ | $R$ | $\left(\dfrac{-\pi}{2}, \dfrac{\pi}{2}\right)$ |
| $y = \cot^{-1}x$ | $R$ | $(0, \pi)$ |

*Note:*

$\sin^{-1}x \neq (\sin x)^{-1}$

$(\sin x)^{-1} = \dfrac{1}{\sin x}$

The other five trigononometric functions are also defined in a similar manner.

The value of an inverse trigonometric function which lies in its principal value branch is called the principal value of that inverse trigonometric function.

Whenever no branch of an inverse trigonometric function is mentioned, we mean the principal value branch of that function.

For suitable values of domain,

- $y = \sin^{-1}x \Rightarrow x = \sin y$
- $x = \sin y \Rightarrow y = \sin^{-1}x$
- $\sin(\sin^{-1}x) = x$
- $\sin^{-1}(\sin x) = x$

- $\sin^{-1}\dfrac{1}{x} = \mathrm{cosce}^{-1}x$

- $\cos^{-1}\dfrac{1}{x} = \sec^{-1}x$

- $\tan^{-1}\dfrac{1}{x} = \cot^{-1}x$

- $\sin^{-1}(-x) = -\sin^{-1}x$
- $\tan^{-1}(-x) = -\tan^{-1}x$
- $\mathrm{cosec}^{-1}(-x) = -\mathrm{cosec}^{-1}x$
- $\cos^{-1}(-x) = \pi - \cos^{-1}x$
- $\cot^{-1}(-x) = \pi - \cot^{-1}x$
- $\sec^{-1}(-x) = \pi - \sec^{-1}x$

- $\sin^{-1}x + \cos^{-1}x = \dfrac{\pi}{2}$

- $\tan^{-1}x + \cot^{-1}x = \dfrac{\pi}{2}$

- $\mathrm{cosec}^{-1}x + \sec^{-1}x = \dfrac{\pi}{2}$

- $\tan^{-1}x + \tan^{-1}y = \tan^{-1}\dfrac{x+y}{1-xy}$

- $\tan^{-1}x - \tan^{-1}y = \tan^{-1}\dfrac{x-y}{1+xy}$

- $2\tan^{-1}x = \tan^{-1}\dfrac{2x}{1-x^2}$

- $2\tan^{-1}x = \sin^{-1}\dfrac{2x}{1+x^2} = \cos^{-1}\dfrac{1-x^2}{1+x^2}$

Maths Formulae For School Students

# Graph of Trigonometric Functions

$y = \sin x$

$y = \sin^{-1}x$

$y = \cos x$

$y = \cos^{-1}x$

$y = \tan x$

$y = \tan^{-1}x$

$y = cosec\, x$

$y = cosec^{-1}x$

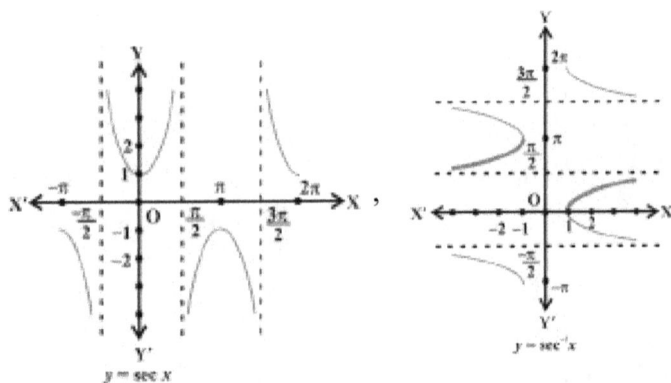

$y = \sec x$

$y = \sec^{-1}x$

Maths Formulae For School Students

$y = \cot x$

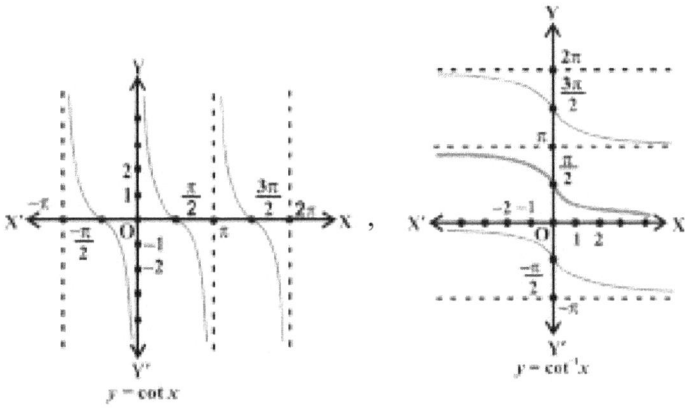

$y = \cot^{-1} x$

## Angle of Elevation and Depression

The *angle of elevation* of an object as seen by an observer is the angle between the horizontal and the line from the object to the observer's eye (line of sight). In this case the object is above the level of the observer.

If the object is below the observer, then the angle between the horizontal and the line of sight of the observer is known as the *angle of depression*.

Using trigonometric ratios we can determine the height or length of an object or the distance between two distant objects.

# (5)

## *Coordinate Geometry Formulae*

### ═══ MENSURATION ═══

## Area and Perimeter of 2D Shapes

| Name of Shape | Shape | Formula |
|---|---|---|
| Square | | Perimeter = 4 × s<br>Area = s × s |
| Rectangle | | Perimeter $2l$ + 2w<br>Area = $l$ × w |
| Parallelogram | | Perimeter = $2l$ + 2b<br>Area = base × height |
| Rhombus | | Perimeter = 4 × a<br>Area = $(d_1 × d_2)/2$ |
| Triangle | | Perimeter = a + b + c<br>Area = (b × h)/2 |
| Equilateral Triangle | | Perimeter = 3 × a<br>Area = $(\sqrt{3}a^2)/4$ |
| Trapezoid | | Perimeter = sum of all sides<br>Area = (a + b) x h/2 |
| Circle | | Circumference = 2 x π x r<br>Area = π x $r^2$ |
| Semicircle | | Circumference = π x r x D<br>Area = $(\pi r^2)/2$ |

## Useful Formula for Fencing Problems

Length of the fence = Total cost of fencing ÷ Rate

## Heron's Formula

### Area of Triangle

If $a$, $b$, $c$ are three sides of a triangle, then area of triangle by Heron's formula is given by

Area of triangle = $\sqrt{s(s-a)(s-b)(s-c)}$  where  $s = \dfrac{a+b+c}{2}$

### Area of Quadrilateral

Area of a quadrilateral whose one diagonal and the sides are given, can be calculated by dividing the quadrilateral into two triangles and using the Heron's formula.

## Area and Length of a Sector

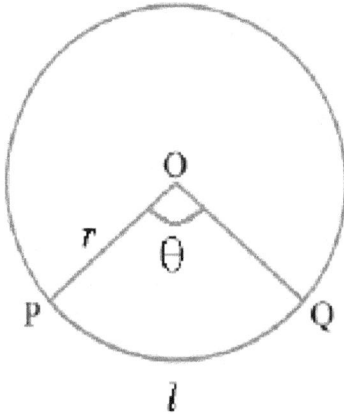

If $r$ is the radius of a circle and $\theta$ is the sector angle, then the area of the sectors and the length of the arc are given by

Area of minor sector = $\dfrac{\theta}{360} \times \pi r^2$

Area of major sector = $\pi r^2$ – Area of minor sector

Length of arc = $\dfrac{\theta}{360} \times 2\pi r$

# Area of a Segment

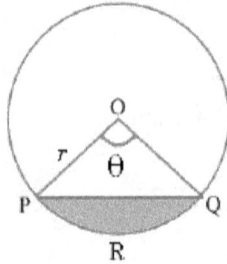

If $r$ is the radius of a circle and $\theta$ is the sector angle, then the area of the minor segment is given by

Area of minor segment PRQ

= Area of minor sector OPRQ – Area of triangle POQ

Area of major segment = $\pi r^2$ – Area of minor segment

# Area and Volume of Cube and Cuboid

| S. No. | Name | Figure | Total Surface Area (sq.units) | Curved Surface Area (sq.units) | Volume (cu.units) |
|--------|------|--------|------------------------------|-------------------------------|-------------------|
| 1. | Cube | $a$ | $6a^2$ | $4a^2$ | $a^3$ <br> Diagonal $= \sqrt{3}\, a$ |
| 2. | Cuboid | $h$ <br> $l$ $b$ | $2(lb + bh + hl)$ | $2h(l + b)$ | $l \times b \times h$ <br> Diagonal $= \sqrt{l^2 + b^2 + h^2}$ |

# Area and Volume of Cylinder, Cone, Sphere and Hemisphere

| S. No. | Name | Figure | Lateral or Curved Surface Area (sq. units) | Total Surface Area (sq. units) | Volume (cu. units) |
|--------|------|--------|-------------------------------------------|-------------------------------|-------------------|
| 1. | Solid right circular cylinder | | $2\pi rh$ | $2\pi r(h + r)$ | $\pi r^2 h$ |
| 2. | Right circular hollow cylinder | | $2\pi h(R + r)$ | $2\pi h(R + r)$ <br> $(R - r + h)$ | $\pi R^2 h - \pi r^2 h$ <br> $\pi h(R^2 - r^2)$ <br> $\pi h(R + r)(R - r)$ |

| 3. | Solid right circular cone | | $\pi r l$ | $\pi r(l + r)$ | $\dfrac{1}{3}\pi r^2 h$ |
|---|---|---|---|---|---|
| 4. | Frustum | | $\pi l(R + r)$ | $\pi l(R + r)$ $+\pi(R^2 + r^2)$ $l = \sqrt{h^2 + (R-r)^2}$ | $\dfrac{1}{3}\pi h(R^2 + r^2 + Rr)$ |
| 5. | Sphere | | $4\pi r^2$ | --- | $\dfrac{4}{3}\pi r^3$ |
| 6. | Hollow sphere | | ... | ... | $\dfrac{4}{3}\pi(R^3 - r^3)$ |
| 7. | Solid Hemishere | | $2\pi r^2$ | $3\pi r^2$ | $\dfrac{2}{3}\pi r^3$ |
| 8. | Hollow Hemishere | | $2\pi(R^2 + r^2)$ | $2\pi(R^2 + r^2)$ $+ \pi(R^2 - r^2)$ | $\dfrac{2}{3}\pi(R^3 - r^3)$ |

| 9. | A sector of a circle converted into a Cone CSA of cone = Area of sector $$\pi r l = \dfrac{\theta}{360} \times \pi r^2$$ Length of the sector = Base circumference of the cone $l = \sqrt{h^2 + r^2}$ $h = \sqrt{l^2 - r^2}$ $r = \sqrt{l^2 - h^2}$ | 10. Volume of water flows out through a pipe = {Cross section area × Speed × Time} 11. No. of new solids obtained by recasting $= \dfrac{\text{Volume of the solid which is melted}}{\text{volume of one solid which is made}}$ |
|---|---|---|

| 12. | Conversions 1m$^3$ = 1000 litres, 1m$^3$ = 1 litre, 1000 cm$^3$ = 1 litre, 1000 litres = 1k$l$ |
|---|---|

To locate the position of a point in a plane, we require two perpendicular lines. One of them is horizontal and the other is vertical.

The plane is called the **Cartesian plane** or the **coordinate plane** and the lines are known as the axes. The horizontal line is known as the $x$ axis and the vertical line is known as the $y$ axis.

The point where the $x$ axis and $y$ axis intersect is known as the **origin**.

Two numbers written in a certain order are known as an **ordered pair**. For example, while writing the coordinates of any point in cartesian plane( coordinate plane) we write the $x$ -coordinate first and then the $y$-coordinate i.e. in the form of $(x,y)$. $x$ coordinate is known as **abscissa** and the $y$ coordinate is known as **ordinate**.

- The ordered pair $(x,y) = (y,x)$ if $x = y$
- The ordered pair $(x,y) \neq (y,x)$ if $x \neq y$
- Coordinates of origin $= (0,0)$
- Coordinates of any point on the $x$-axis $= (x, 0)$ or $(-x, 0)$
- Coordinates of any point on the $y$-axis $= (0, y)$ or $(0, -y)$

## Distance Formula

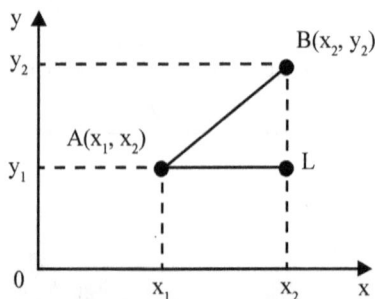

The distance between two points A $(x_1, y_1)$ and B$(x_2, y_2)$ is given by:

$$AB = \sqrt{(x_2 - x_1)^2 + (y_2 - y_1)^2}$$

## Distance from Origin

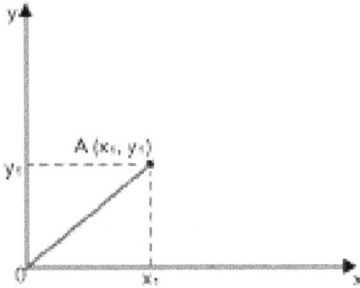

The distance of the point A $(x_1, y_1)$ from the origin is given by:

$$OA = \sqrt{x_1^2 + y_1^2}$$

## Mid Point Formula

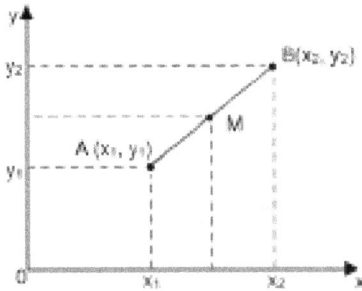

The mid point M of the line segment joining A $(x_1, y_1)$ and B$(x_2, y_2)$ is given by:

$$\left( \frac{x_1 + x_2}{2}, \frac{y_1 + y_2}{2} \right)$$

## Section Formula

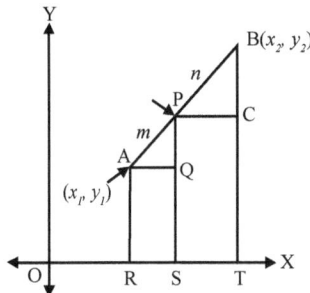

The coordinates of the point P$(x,y)$ which divides the line segment joining the points A $(x_1, y_1)$ and B$(x_2, y_2)$ *internally* in the ratio *m: n* is given by:

$$\left( \frac{mx_2 + nx_1}{m+n}, \frac{my_2 + my_1}{m+n} \right)$$

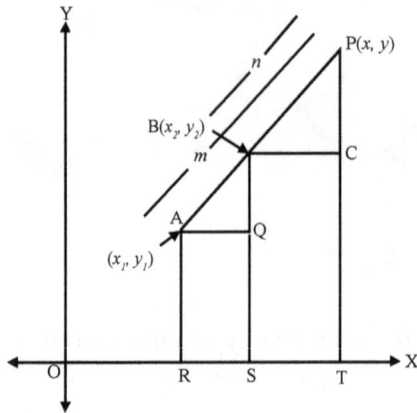

The coordinates of the point P$(x, y)$ which divides the line segment joining the points A $(x_1, y_1)$ and B$(x_2, y_2)$ *externally* in the ratio *m: n* is given by

$$\left( \frac{mx_2 - nx_1}{m-n}, \frac{my_2 - ny_1}{m-n} \right)$$

## Area of a Triangle

The area of the triangle formed by the points A $(x_1, y_1)$, B$(x_2, y_2)$ and C $(x_3, y_3)$ is given by the numerical value of the expression:

$$\frac{1}{2} [x_1(y_2 - y_3) + x_2(y_3 - y_1) + x_3(y_1 - y_2)]$$

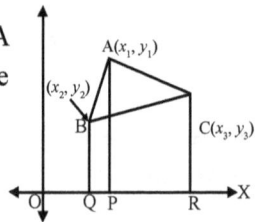

=== STRAIGHT LINE ===

## Slope

- In a coordinate plane a straight line forms two angles with the *x*-axis which are supplementary.
- The angle θ made by the line *l* with positive direction of *x*-axis and measured anti clockwise is called the **inclination of the line** ($0° \leq \theta \leq 180°$).
- The inclination of a horizontal line (co-

inciding with $x$ axis or parallel to $x$ axis is 0°. The inclination of a vertical line (coinciding with $y$ axis or parallel to $y$ axis) is 90°.

- If $\theta$ is the inclination of a line $l$, then
  Gradient of line $l$ = Slope($m$) = tan $\theta$, where $\theta \neq 90°$
- Slope of $x$-axis is zero and slope of $y$-axis is not defined.

## Slope of a Line when Coordinates of Any Two Points on the Line are Given

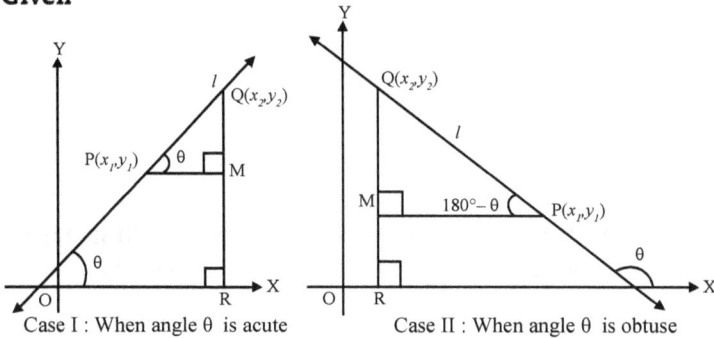

Case I : When angle $\theta$ is acute

Case II : When angle $\theta$ is obtuse

In both the cases(the angle is acute and obtuse) the slope $m$ of the line $l$ through the points $(x_1, y_1)$ and $(x_2, y_2)$ is given by:

$$m = \frac{y_2 - y_1}{x_2 - x_1} \text{ where } x_1 \neq x_2$$

## Condition for Lines to be Parallel

Two non vertical lines $l_1$ and $l_2$ are parallel if and only if their slopes $m_1$ and $m_2$ are equal.

$$\text{or tan } \alpha = \text{tan } \beta$$

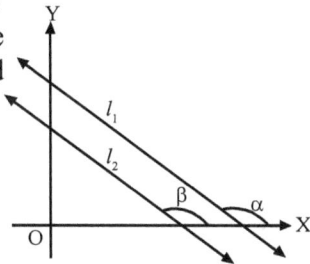

## Condition for Lines to be Perpendicular

Two non vertical lines $l_1$ and $l_2$ are perpendicular to each other if and only if their slopes $m_1$ and $m_2$ are negative reciprocals of each other.

$$m_2 = -\frac{1}{m_1} \text{ or, } m_1 m_2 = -1$$

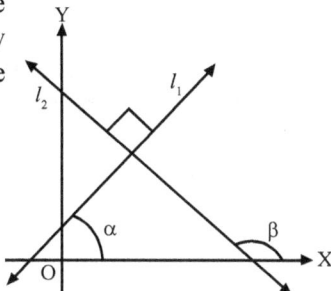

# Angle Between Two Lines

If $\theta$ be the acute angle between two lines $L_1$ and $L_2$ with slopes $m_1$ and $m_2$ respectively, then angle between the lines is given by

$$\tan \theta = \left| \frac{m_2 - m_1}{1 + m_2 m_1} \right|, \text{ where } 1 + m_1 m_2 \neq 0$$

The obtuse angle $\varphi = 180° - \theta$

## Collinearity of Three Points
Three points A, B and C are collinear if and only if
Slope of AB = Slope of BC

## Equation of Vertical Line
The equation of a vertical line at a distance $a$ is given by either $x = a$ or $x = -a$

# Equation of Horizontal Line

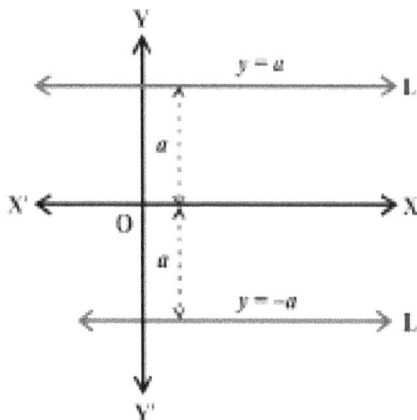

The equation of a horizontal line at a distance $a$ is given by either $y = a$ or $y = -a$.

# Point Slope Form

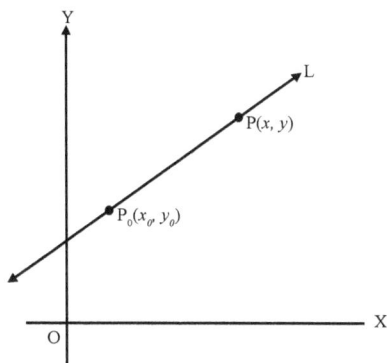

The point $(x, y)$ lies on the line L with slope $m$ through the fixed point $(x_0, y_0)$, if and only if, its coordinates satisfy the equation

$$y - y_0 = m(x - x_0)$$

# Two Point Form

Equation of the line passing through points $(x_1, y_1)$ and $(x_2, y_2)$ is given by

$$y - y_1 = \frac{y_2 - y_1}{x_2 - x_1}(x - x_1)$$

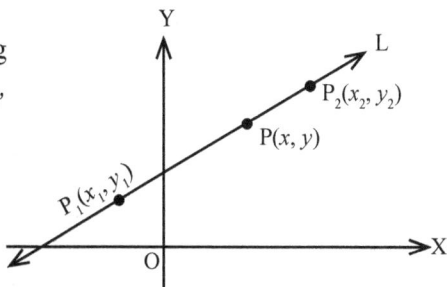

## Slope Intercept Form

The point $(x, y)$ on the line with slope $m$ and $x$-intercept $d$ lies on the line if and only if $y = m(x - d)$.

The point $(x, y)$ on the line with slope $m$ and $y$-intercept $c$ lies on the line if and only if $y = mx + c$ ($c$ is positive or negative depending on the direction of the intercept i.e positive or negative side of the $y$ axis).

## Intercept Form

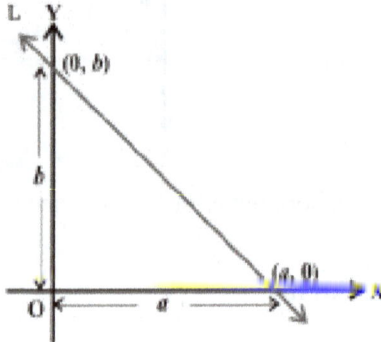

Equation of a line making intercepts $a$ and $b$ on the $x$ axis and $y$ axis respectively is given by

$$\frac{x}{a} + \frac{y}{b} = 1$$

## Normal Form

Let the normal distance (OA) of line L from the origin be $p$ and let the angle between the normal and the positive $x$ axis be $\omega$ then the equation of the line is given by

$$x \cos \omega + y \sin \omega = p$$

## General Equation of a Line

Any equation of the form $Ax + By + C = 0$, where A and B are not zero simultaneously, is called the general equation of a line.

(iii) *Generator* : The line (other than the central axis) joining the base of a cone to its vertex or apex is known as generator.

(iv) *Vertex* : A cone tapers from a flat base to a point. This point is known as apex or vertex of the cone.

(v) *Central Axis* : The axis of symmetry of a right circular cone is known as central axis.

## Sections of a Cone

Let $\alpha$ be the angle between the generator and the central axis of a cone and $\beta$ be the angle between the central axis of the cone and the intersecting plane.

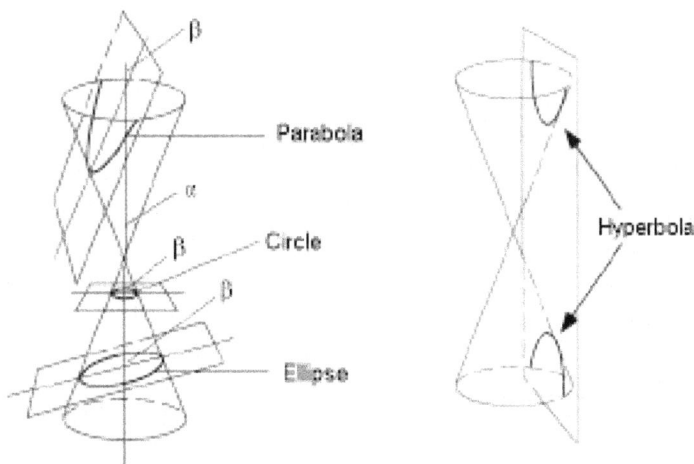

(i) *Circle* : If a plane is perpendicular to the central axis of the cone i.e. if $\beta = 90°$, the section of the cone is known as a circle.

(ii) *Parabola* : If a plane is not perpendicular to the central axis of the cone and if $\alpha = \beta$, the section of the cone is known as a parabola.

(iii) *Ellipse* : If a plane is not perpendicular to the central axis of the cone and if $\alpha < \beta < 90°$, the section of the cone is known as an ellipse.

(iv) *Hyperbola* : If a plane intersects both the nappes of a cone i.e. when $0 \leq \beta < \alpha$, the section of the cone is known as a hyperbola.

=========== **PARABOLA** ===========

*Focus and Directrix* : The set of all points in a plane that are equidistant from a fixed line and a fixed point (not on the line) in the plane is known as a parabola. The fixed point is called the focus and the fixed line is called the directrix.

*Axis* : A line perpendicular to the directrix which passes through the focus is called the axis of the parabola.

*Vertex* : The point of intersection of parabola with the axis is known as the vertex of the parabola.

*Latus Rectum* : A line segment whose end points lie on the parabola and which is perpendicular to the axis of the parabola through the focus is known as the latus rectum of the parabola.

## Different Orientations of a Parabola

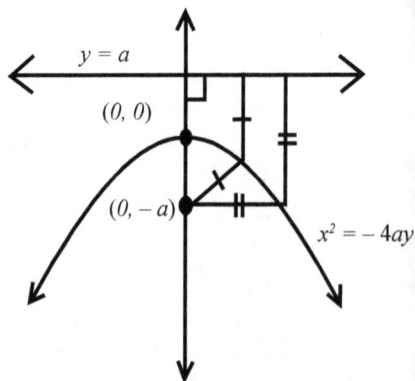

$x^2 = 4ax$

$x^2 = -4ax$

$x = -a$

$x = a$

$(0, 0)$ $(a, 0)$

$(-a, 0)$ $(0, 0)$

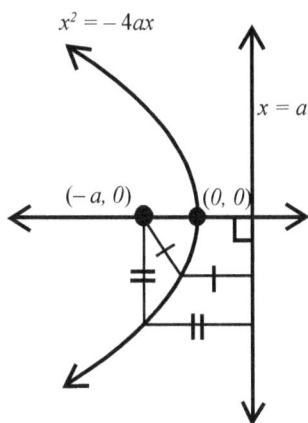

## Properties of Parabola

| Standard Equation | $x^2 = 4ay$ $(a > 0)$ Upward | $x^2 = -4ay$ $(a > 0)$ Downward | $y^2 = 4ax$ $(a > 0)$ Rightside | $y^2 = -4ax$ $(a > 0)$ Leftside |
|---|---|---|---|---|
| Directrix | $y = -a$ | $y = a$ | $x = -a$ | $x = a$ |
| Axis | $x = 0$ | $x = 0$ | $y = 0$ | $y = 0$ |
| Vertex | $(0,0)$ | $(0,0)$ | $(0,0)$ | $(0,0)$ |
| Focus | $(0,a)$ | $(0, -a)$ | $(a,0)$ | $(-a,0)$ |
| Focal distance of the point $(x,y)$ | $a + y$ | $a - y$ | $a + x$ | $a - x$ |
| Tangent at the vertex | $y = 0$ | $y = 0$ | $x = 0$ | $x = 0$ |
| Length of latus rectum | 4a | 4a | 4a | 4a |

An ellipse is the set of all points in a plane, the sum of whose distances from two fixed points in the plane is a constant and is equal to the major axis.

$$P_1F + P_1F' = P_2F + P_2F' = P_3F + P_3F' = \text{constant} = 2a \, (> FF')$$

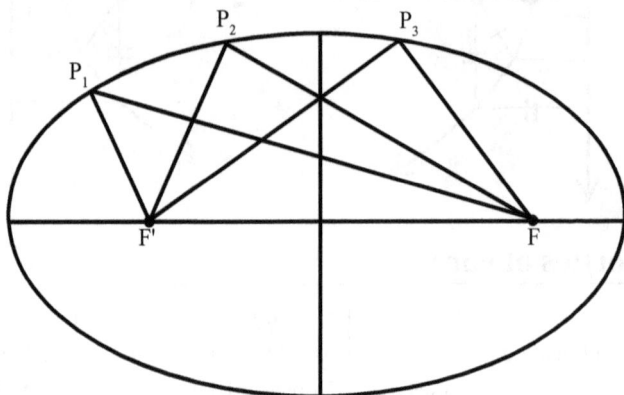

Each fixed point is known as the *focus* of an ellipse. In the above figure F and F' represents the foci.

*Centre* : The mid point of the line segment joining the two foci is known as the centre (O) of the ellipse.

*Major Axis* : The line segment which passes through the two foci and whose end points lie on the ellipse is known as the major axis(AB). Length of the major axis is represented by *2a*.

*Semi Major Axis:* Half of major axis is known as semi major axis (AO or BO). Length of the semi major axis is represented by *a*.

*Minor Axis* : The line segment which passes through the centre and is perpendicular to the major axis is known as the minor axis (CD). Length of the minor axis is represented by *2b*.

*Semi Minor Axis* : Half of minor axis is known as semi minor axis (CO or DO). Length of the semi minor axis is represented by *b*.

*Vertices* : The end points of the major axis are known as the vertices of the ellipse. In the above figure points A and B represent the vertices.

## Relationship between Semi-major Axis, Semi-minor Axis and the Distance of the Focus From the Centre of the Ellipse

If the length of the semi major axis, semi minor axis and the distance between the centre and the focus is *a, b* and *c* respectively, then

$$2\sqrt{b^2 + c^2} = 2a \text{ or } c = \sqrt{a^2 - b^2}$$

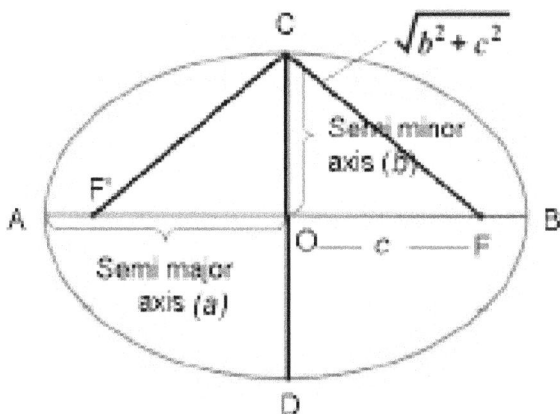

*Special Cases*

(i) If $c = 0$, *a* becomes equal to *b* and the ellipse reduces to a circle.

(ii) If $c = a$, then *b* becomes equal to 0 and the ellipse reduces to a line segment.

## Eccentricity of an Ellipse

Eccentricity is a measure of how much the conic section deviates from being circular.

The eccentricity of an ellipse is the ratio of the distances from the centre of the ellipse to one of the foci and to one of the vertices of the ellipse. Eccentricity is represented by $e$ and is given by $e = \dfrac{c}{a}$

*Note*:

For an ellipse $e < 1$, for a circle $e = 0$, for a parabola $e = 1$ and for hyperbola $e > 1$.

## Standard Equation of an Ellipse

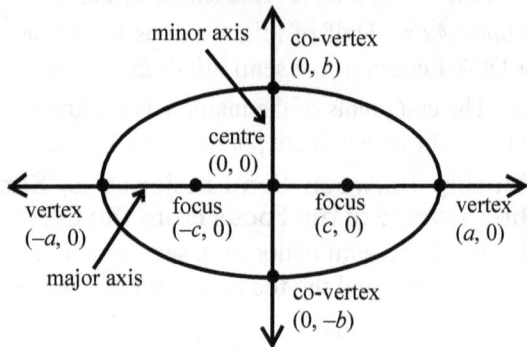

The equation of the ellipse with horizontal(along $x$ axis) major axis and passing through the centre is given by $\dfrac{x^2}{a^2} + \dfrac{y^2}{b^2} = 1$

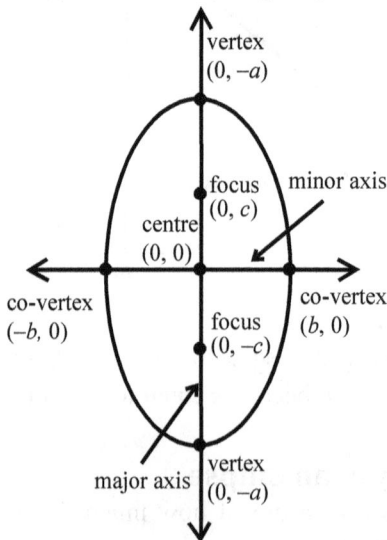

The equation of the ellipse with vertcal(along $y$ axis) major axis and passing through the centre is given by $\dfrac{x^2}{b^2} + \dfrac{y^2}{a^2} = 1$

# Latus Rectum

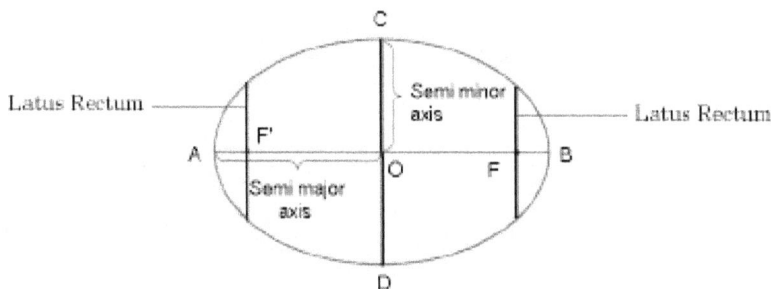

A line segment passing through any of the foci and perpendicular to the major axis is known as the latus rectum of an ellipse. The end points of the latus rectum lie on the ellipse.

## Directrix and Focal Radius

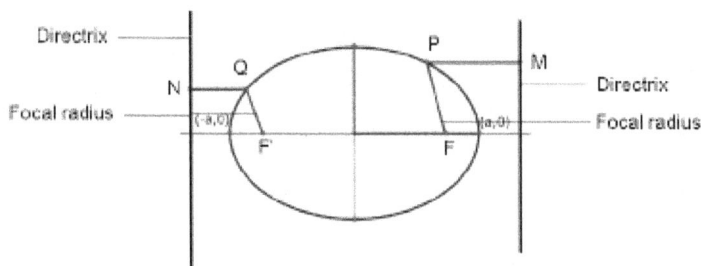

*Directrix* : It is a line parallel to the minor axis such that the distance from any point(P or Q) on the ellipse to the focus( F or F') is a constant fraction of that point's perpendicular distance (M or N) to the directrix, resulting in the equality

$$e = \frac{PF}{PM} \text{ or } e = \frac{QF'}{QN}$$

*Focal Radius* : The distance from a focus to a point on the ellipse is called focal radius (PF or QF').

## Properties of Ellipse
1. Ellipse is symmetric with respect to both the coordinate axes.
2. The foci of an ellipse always lie on the major axis.
3. The sum of focal radii is constant (PF + PF' = 2a or QF + QF' = 2a)

| Standard Equation | $\dfrac{x^2}{a^2}+\dfrac{y^2}{b^2}=1$ (Horizontal major axis) | $\dfrac{x^2}{b^2}+\dfrac{y^2}{a^2}=1$ (Vertical major axis) |
|---|---|---|
| Length of major axis | $2a$ | $2a$ |
| Length of minor axis | $2b$ | $2b$ |
| Equation of major axis | $y=0$ | $x=0$ |
| Equation of minor axis | $x=0$ | $y=0$ |
| Centre | $(0,0)$ | $(0,0)$ |
| Vertices | $(\pm a, 0)$ | $(0, \pm a)$ |
| Foci | $(\pm ae, 0)$ | $(0, \pm ae)$ |
| Distance between two foci | $2ae$ | $2ae$ |
| Eccentricity | $e=\dfrac{\sqrt{a^2-b^2}}{a}$ | $e=\dfrac{\sqrt{a^2-b^2}}{a}$ |
| Length of latus rectum | $\dfrac{2b^2}{a}$ | $\dfrac{2b^2}{a}$ |
| Equation of directrix | $x=\pm\dfrac{a}{e}$ | $y=\pm\dfrac{a}{e}$ |
| Distance between two directrix | $x=\dfrac{2a}{e}$ | $x=\dfrac{2a}{e}$ |
| Equation of tangent at the vertex | $x=\pm a$ | $y=\pm a$ |

## Parametric Coordinates

For the ellipse,

$$\frac{x^2}{a^2}+\frac{y^2}{b^2}=1 \ \text{ or } \ \frac{x^2}{b^2}+\frac{y^2}{a^2}=1$$

the parametric coordinates are given by $x = a\cos\theta$, $y = b\sin\theta$ where $0° \le \theta < 360°$

## Auxillary Circle

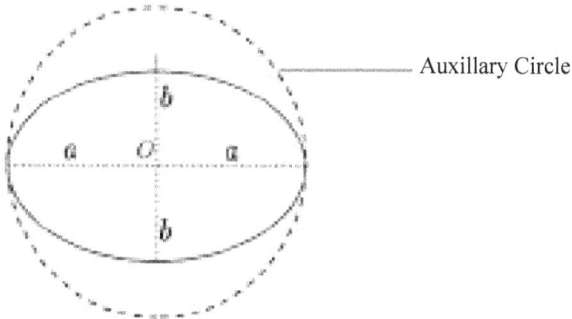

Auxillary Circle

The circle drawn with major axis as the diameter is known as an auxillary circle.

## ═══ HYPERBOLA ═══

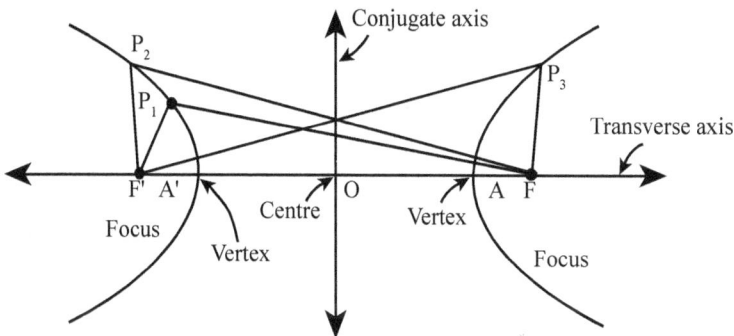

The set of all points in a plane, the difference of whose distances from two fixed points in the plane is a constant, is known as a hyperbola.

$P_1F - P_1F' = P_2F - P_2F' = P_3F' - P_3F = $ constant $= 2a$

The two fixed points(F and F') are called the *foci* of the hyperbola.

*Centre* : The mid point of the line segment joining the two foci is known as the centre (O) of the hyperbola.

*Transverse Axis* : The line passing through the two foci is known as the transverse axis.

*Conjugate Axis* : The line which passes through the centre and is perpendicular to the transverse axis is known as the conjugate axis.

*Vertex* : The points at which the hyperbola intersects the transverse axis are known as the vertices(A and A') of the hyperbola.

## Eccentricity

Like an ellipse, the eccentricity of the hyperbola is given by $e = \dfrac{c}{a}$

For a hyperbola, $e > 1$.

The foci are at a distance of $ae$ from the centre in terms of eccentricity.

## Standard Equation of Hyperbola

The equation of the hyperbola with focus on the $x$ axis and passing through the centre is given by

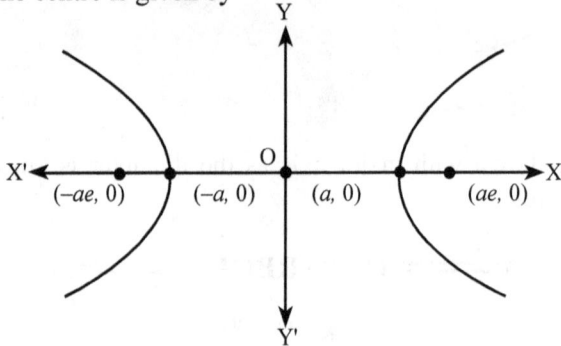

$$\frac{x^2}{a^2} - \frac{y^2}{b^2} = 1$$

The equation of the hyperbola with focus on the $y$ axis and passing through the centre is given by

$$\frac{x^2}{a^2} - \frac{y^2}{b^2} = -1$$

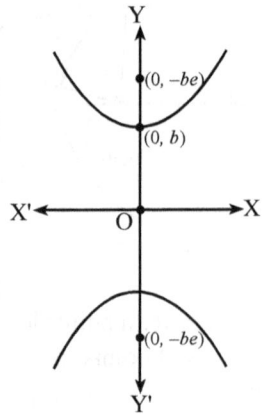

*Equilateral Hyperbola* : A hyperbola in which $a = b$ is known as an equilateral hyperbola.

## Latus Rectum

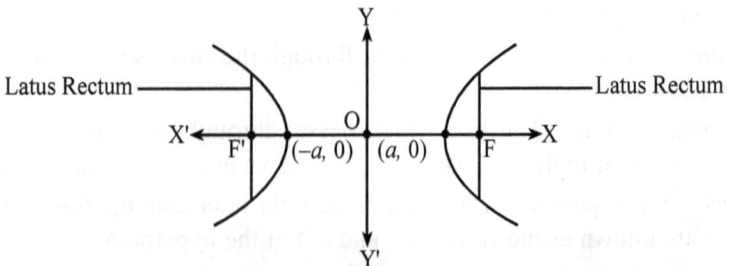

A line segment passing through any of the foci and perpendicular to the transverse axis is known as the latus rectum of a hyperbola. The end points of the latus rectum lie on the hyperbola.

## Directrix

Directrix is a line parallel to the conjugate axis such that the distance from any point(P or P') on the hyperbola to the focus( F or F') is a constant fraction of that point's perpendicular distance (M or M') to the directrix, resulting in the equality

$$e = \frac{PF}{PM} \text{ or } e = \frac{P'F'}{P'M'}$$

## Properties of Hyperbola
1. Hyperbola is symmetric with respect to both the axes.
2. The foci are always on the transverse axis.

|  | Hyperbola (Focus on $x$ axis) | Conjugate Hyperbola (Focus on $y$ axis) |
|---|---|---|
| Standard Equation | $\frac{x^2}{a^2} - \frac{y^2}{b^2} = 1$ | $\frac{x^2}{a^2} - \frac{y^2}{b^2} = -1$ |
| Length of transverse axis | $2a$ | $2b$ |
| Length of conjugate axis | $2b$ | $2a$ |
| Equation of transverse axis | $y = 0$ | $x = 0$ |
| Equation of conjugate axis | $x = 0$ | $y = 0$ |

| Centre | (0,0) | (0,0) |
|---|---|---|
| Vertices | (±a, 0) | (0 ± b) |
| Foci | (± ae, 0) | (0, ± be) |
| Difference of focal radii | 2a | 2b |
| Eccentricity | $e = \dfrac{\sqrt{a^2 + b^2}}{a}$ | $e = \dfrac{\sqrt{a^2 + b^2}}{b}$ |
| Length of latus rectum | $\dfrac{2b^2}{a}$ | $\dfrac{2a^2}{b}$ |
| Equation of directrix | $x = \pm\dfrac{a}{e}$ | $y = \pm\dfrac{b}{e}$ |
| Equation of tangent at the vertex | $x = \pm a$ | $y = \pm b$ |

## Parametric Coordinates

(i) For the hyperbola, $\dfrac{x^2}{a^2} - \dfrac{y^2}{b^2} = 1$

the parametric coordinates are given by $x = a\sec\theta, y = b\tan\theta$
where $0° \le \theta < 360°$

(ii) For the hyperbola, $\dfrac{x^2}{a^2} - \dfrac{y^2}{b^2} = -1$

the parametric coordinates are given by $x = b\sec\theta, y = a\tan\theta$
where $0° \le \theta < 360°$

=== **CIRCLE** ===

## Definition

A set of points in a plane that are equidistant from a fixed point in the plane is called a circle.

## Standard Equation of a Circle

If $P(x,y)$ is any point on a circle with centre $C(h,k)$ and radius r then the equation of the circle is given by

$$(x - h)^2 + (y - k)^2 = r^2$$

*Equation of a Circle from the Origin*

If $P(x,y)$ is any point on a circle with centre at the origin and radius r then the equation of the circle is given by

$$x^2 + y^2 = r^2$$

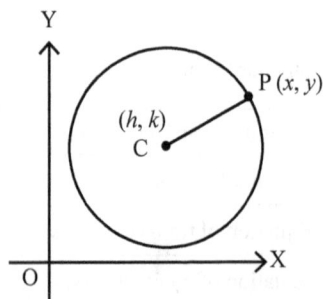

# General Equation of a Circle

The equation of a circle with centre $(-g, -f)$ and radius $\sqrt{g^2 + f^2 - c}$ is given by $x^2 + y^2 + 2gx + 2fy + c = 0$ where $g$, $f$ and $c$ are constants.

## Conditions for an Equation to represent a Circle

A general equation of second degree
$ax^2 + 2hxy + by^2 + 2gx + 2fy + c = 0$ in $x$, $y$ represents a circle if
  (i) $2h = 0$ (Coefficient of $xy = 0$)
  (ii) $a = b$ (Coefficient of $x^2 = y^2$)

## Nature of Circle

  (i) If $g^2 + f^2 - c > 0$, then the general equation represents real circle with centre at $(-g, -f)$.
  (ii) If $g^2 + f^2 - c = 0$, then the general equation represents a point circle (radius zero).
  (iii) If $g^2 + f^2 - c < 0$, then the general equation represents an imaginary circle (centre is real but radius is imaginary).

# Different Forms of Equation of a Circle
## Circle Touching the x Axis

The equation of the circle touching the $x$ axis and with centre $C(h, k)$ is given by

$$(x - h)^2 + (y - k)^2 = k^2$$

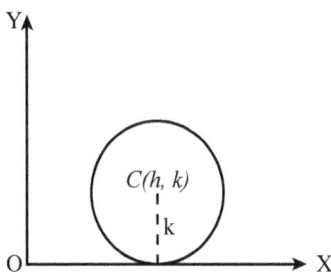

## Circle Touching the y Axis

The equation of the circle touching the $y$ axis and with centre $C(h, k)$ is given by

$$(x - h)^2 + (y - k)^2 = h^2$$

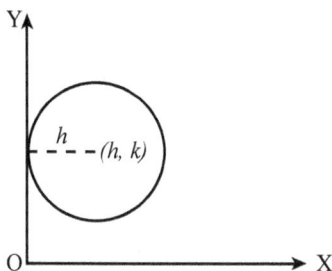

## Circle Touching Both $x$ and $y$ Axis

The equation of the circle touching both the coordinate axis and having radius $g$ is given by

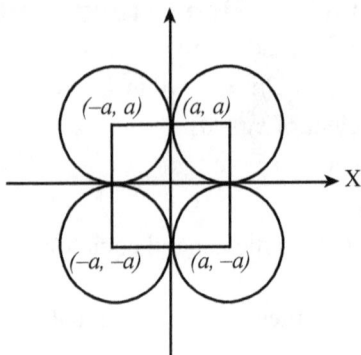

$$(x \pm a)^2 + (y \pm a)^2 = a^2$$

## Equation of a Circle in Diametric Form

If $A(x_1, y_1)$ and $B(x_2, y_2)$ are the end points of a diameter, then the equation of the circle is given by

$$(x - x_1)(x - x_2) + (y - y_1)(y - y_2) = 0$$

Centre $= \left( \dfrac{x_1 + x_2}{2}, \dfrac{y_1 + y_2}{2} \right)$

Radius $= \sqrt{\left( \dfrac{x_1 - x_2}{2} \right)^2 + \left( \dfrac{y_1 - y_2}{2} \right)^2}$

## Intercepts Made by a Circle on the Coordinate Axes

(i) Intercepts are always positive.

(ii) The length of the intercept made by the circle
$x^2 + y^2 + 2gx + 2fy + c = 0$ on

$x$ axis $= 2\sqrt{g^2 - c}$ and $y$ axis $= 2\sqrt{f^2 - c}$

(iii) If the circle touches $x$ axis, then $c = g^2$

(iv) If the circle touches $y$ axis, then $c = f^2$

(v) If the circle touches both the coordinate axes, then $c = g^2 = f^2$

## Parametric Equation of a Circle

Let $P(x, y)$ be any point on the circle with centre at the origin and radius $a$. Let OP make an angle $\theta$ with the $x$ axis, then

(i) the parametric equation of the circle $x^2 + y^2 = a^2$ is

$x = a \cos \theta,$

$y = a \sin \theta,$ where $0° \leq \theta \leq 360°$

*Note:* The parametric equation of the circle

$(x - h)^2 + (y - k)^2 = r^2$ is $x = h + r \cos \theta$ and $y = k + r \sin \theta$

## Position of a point with respect to a circle

Let $P(x_1, y_1)$ be a point on the circle

$x^2 + y^2 + 2gx + 2fy + c = 0$, then

(i) the point lies on the circle if $x_1^2 + y_1^2 + 2gx_1 + 2fy_1 + c = 0$

(ii) the point lies outside the circle if $x_1^2 + y_1^2 + 2gx_1 + 2fy_1 + c > 0$

(iii) the point lies inside the circle if $x_1^2 + y_1^2 + 2gx_1 + 2fy_1 + c < 0$

## Equation of a Circle through Three non Collinear Points

If $A(x_1, y_1)$, $B(x_2, y_2)$ and $C(x_3, y_3)$ are three non collinear points, then the equation of the circle through these three points is given by

$$\begin{vmatrix} x^2 + y^2 & x & y & 1 \\ x_1^2 + y_1^2 & x_1 & y_1 & 1 \\ x_2^2 + y_2^2 & x_2 & y_2 & 1 \\ x_3^2 + y_3^2 & x_3 & y_3 & 1 \end{vmatrix} = 0$$

## Contact between Two Circles

If $A(x_1, y_1)$ and $B(x_2, y_2)$ be the centre of two circles with radii $r_1$ and $r_2$ respectively, then –

(i) The circles will intersect at two real and distinct points if and only if

$\left| r_1 - r_2 \right| < AB < r_1 + r_2$

(ii) The circles will touch each other internally if and only if

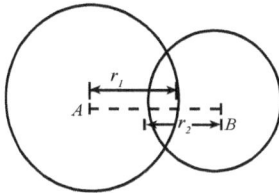

$AB = \left| r_1 - r_2 \right|$ and

Point of contact $(C) = \left( \dfrac{r_1 x_2 - r_2 x_1}{r_1 - r_2}, \dfrac{r_1 y_2 - r_2 y_1}{r_1 - r_2} \right)$

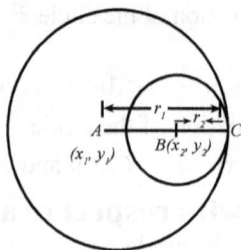

(iii) The circles will touch each other externally if and only if
AB $= r_1 + r_2$ and

Point of contact (C) $= \left( \dfrac{r_1 x_2 + r_2 x_1}{r_1 + r_2}, \dfrac{r_1 y_2 + r_2 y_1}{r_1 + r_2} \right)$

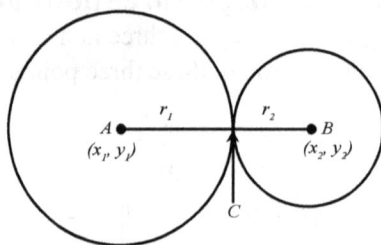

(iv) One circle is contained in the other if AB $< \left| r_1 - r_2 \right|$.

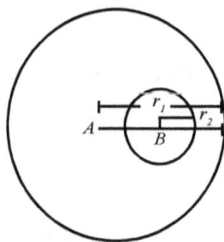

(v) One circle is outside the other circle if AB $> r_1 + r_2$

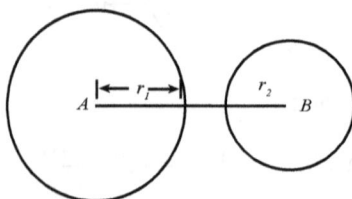

# Equations of Tangent

(i) The equation of a tangent at the point $P(x_1, y_1)$ to the circle $x^2 + y^2 = r^2$ is given by $xx_1 + yy_1 = r^2$

(ii) The equation of a tangent at the point $P(x_1, y_1)$ to the circle $x^2 + y^2 + 2gx + 2fy + c = 0$ is given by

$$xx_1 + yy_1 + g(x + x_1) + f(y + y_1) + c = 0$$

(iii) The equation of a tangent to the circle $x^2 + y^2 = r^2$ with slope $m$

is $y = mx \pm r\sqrt{1 + m^2}$

Coordinates of the point of contact $= \left( \pm \dfrac{rm}{\sqrt{1 + m^2}}, \pm \dfrac{r}{\sqrt{1 + m^2}} \right)$

# Condition of Tangent

- A line will be a tangent to the circle if and only if the perpendicular distance from the centre of the circle to the line is equal to the radius of the circle.

- The straight line $y = mx + c$ will be a tangent to the circle $x^2 + y^2 = r^2$ if $c = \pm r\sqrt{1 + m^2}$

# Length of Tangent

Let $P(x_1, y_1)$ be a point outside the circle $x^2 + y^2 + 2gx + 2fy + c = 0$ then,

Length of tangent $= \sqrt{x_1^2 + y_1^2 + 2gx_1 + 2fy_1 + c}$

# Equation of Pair of Tangent

Let $P(x_1, y_1)$ be a point outside the circle

$$x^2 + y^2 + 2gx + 2fy + c = 0$$

then the equation of the pair of tangent is $SS_1 = T^2$, where

$S = x^2 + y^2 + 2gx + 2fy + c$

$S_1 = x_1^2 + y_1^2 + 2gx_1 + 2fy_1 + c$

$T = xx_1 + yy_1 + g(x + x_1) + f^2(y + y_1) + c$

*Note:* The pair of tangents to the circle $x^2 + y^2 + 2gx + 2fy + c = 0$ from the origin are at right angles if $g^2 + f^2 = 2c$

# Angle of Intersection of Two Circles

The angle between two circles is the angle between their tangents at their point of intersection.

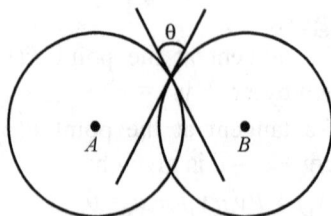

The angle $\theta$ between two circles $x^2 + y^2 + 2g_1x + 2f_1y + c_1$ and $x^2 + y^2 + 2g_2x + 2f_2y + c_2$ is given by

$$\cos\theta = \pm\frac{2g_1g_2 + 2f_1f_2 - c_1 - c_2}{2\sqrt{g_1^2 + f_1^2 - c_1}\cdot\sqrt{g_2^2 + f_2^2 - c_2}}$$

## Orthogonal Intersection of Circles

When two circles intersect at right angles, they are said to intersect orthogonally.

The condition for the two circles $x^2 + y^2 + 2g_1x + 2f_1y + c_1$ and $x^2 + y^2 + 2g_2x + 2f_2y + c_2$ to intersect orthogonally is given by $2g_1g_2 + 2f_1f_2 = c_1 + c_2$

## Equation of a Circle through Two given points

The equation of the circle passing through two given points $A(x_1, y_1)$ and $B(x_2, y_2)$ is given by

$$(x - x_1)(x - x_1) + (y - y_1)(y - y_2) + k\begin{vmatrix} x & y & 1 \\ x_1 & y_1 & 1 \\ x_2 & y_2 & 1 \end{vmatrix} = 0$$

where $k \in R$

## Common Tangents of a Circle

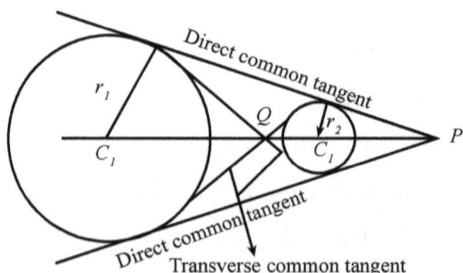

## Direct Common Tangent

The direct common tangent of two circles meet at a point (P) which lies on the line $(C_1C_2)$ joining the centres of the two circles and divide the line joining the two centres externally in the ratio of their radii $(r_1, r_2)$.

## Transverse Common Tangent

The transverse common tangent of two circles meet at a point (Q) which lies on the line $(C_1C_2)$ joining the centres of the two circles and divide the line joining the two centres internally in the ratio of their radii $(r_1, r_2)$.

## =THREE DIMENSIONAL COORDINATE GEOMETRY=

## Rectangular Coordinate System
### Coordinate Axes

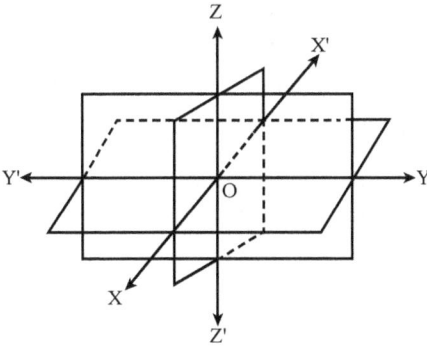

$XOX'$ is called the $x$ axis, $YOY'$ is called the $y$ axis and $ZOZ'$ is called the $z$ axis. The three axis are perpendicular to each other. The three axis together are called coordinate axes.

### Coordinate Plane

The planes XOY, YOZ and ZOX are known as XY-plane, YZ-plane and ZX-plane respectively.

The point O is the origin of the coordinate system.

### Octants

The XY-plane, YZ-plane and ZX-plane divide the space into eight parts known as octants. These octants are named as XOYZ, X'OYZ, X'OY'Z, XOY'Z, XOYZ', X'OYZ', X'OY'Z' and XOY'Z'. They are represented by I, II, III, IV, V, VI, VII and VIII respectively.

## Coordinates of a Point

Let P be any point in space. If we draw perpendicular PM on the XY plane and ML on the $x$ axis then the coordinates of the point P is given by $(x,y,z)$ where $OL = x$, $ML = y$ and $PM = z$.

- The coordinates of the origin $= (0,0,0)$
- The coordinates of any point on the $x$ axis $= (x,0,0)$
- The coordinates of any point on the $y$ axis $= (0,y,0)$
- The coordinates of any point on the $z$ axis $= (0,0,z)$

## Signs of Coordinates in Various Octants

| Octants→ Co-ordinates↓ | I | II | III | IV | V | VI | VII | VIII |
|---|---|---|---|---|---|---|---|---|
| $x$ | + | − | − | + | + | − | − | + |
| $y$ | + | + | − | − | + | + | − | − |
| $z$ | + | + | + | + | − | − | − | − |

## Distance Formula

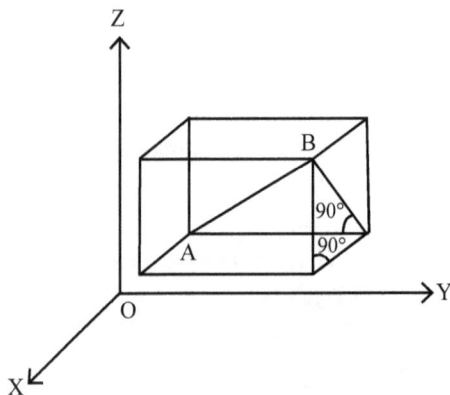

The distance between two points A $(x_1, y_1, z_1)$ and B$(x_2, y_2, z_2)$ is given by

$$AB = \sqrt{(x_2 - x_1)^2 + (y_2 - y_1)^2 + (z_2 - z_1)^2}$$

The distance of a point from the origin is given by $\sqrt{x_2^2 + y_2^2 + z_2^2}$

## Section Formula

(i) The coordinates of the point which divides the line segment joining two points A $(x_1, y_1, z_1)$ and B$(x_2, y_2, z_2)$ internally in the ratio $m : n$ is given by

$$\left( \frac{mx_2 + nx_1}{m+n}, \frac{my_2 + ny_1}{m+n}, \frac{mz_2 + nz_1}{m+n} \right)$$

(ii) The coordinates of the point which divides the line segment joining two points A $(x_1, y_1, z_1)$ and B$(x_2, y_2, z_2)$ externally in the ratio $m : n$ is given by

$$\left( \frac{mx_2 - nx_1}{m-n}, \frac{my_2 - ny_1}{m-n}, \frac{mz_2 - nz_1}{m-n} \right)$$

## Mid Point Formula

(i) The coordinates of the mid point of the line segment joining two points A $(x_1, y_1, z_1)$ and B$(x_2, y_2, z_2)$ is

$$\left( \frac{x_1 + x_2}{2}, \frac{y_1 + y_2}{2}, \frac{z_1 + z_2}{2} \right)$$

(ii) The coordinates of the point which divides the line segment joining two points A $(x_1, y_1, z_1)$ and B$(x_2, y_2, z_2)$ in the ratio $k:1$ is given by

$$\left( \frac{kx_2 + x_1}{1+k}, \frac{ky_2 + y_1}{1+k}, \frac{kz_2 + z_1}{1+k} \right)$$

## Centroid of a Triangle

The coordinates of the centroid of a triangle with vertices A $(x_1, y_1, z_1)$, B$(x_2, y_2, z_2)$ and C $(x_3, y_3, z_3)$ is given by

$$\left( \frac{x_1 + x_2 + x_3}{3}, \frac{y_1 + y_2 + y_3}{3}, \frac{z_1 + z_2 + z_3}{3} \right)$$

=== **LINE IN SPACE** ===

## Direction Cosine and Direction Angle

If a directed line L passing through the origin makes angles α, β and γ with $x$, $y$ and $z$ axes respectively, then

(i) The angles α, β and γ are known as direction angles.

(ii) cos α, cos β and cos γ are known as direction cosines of the directed line L.

(iii) The direction cosines are generally represented by $l$, $m$ and $n$ i.e.
$$l = \cos \alpha, \ m = \cos \beta \text{ and } n = \cos \gamma$$

## Direction Ratio

Any three numbers $a$, $b$, $c$ which are proportional to the direction cosines $l$, $m$, $n$ of a line are known as the direction ratios of the line.

(i) $\dfrac{l}{a} = \dfrac{m}{b} = \dfrac{n}{c} = k \quad k \neq 0, \ k = \text{constant}$

(ii) $l = \pm \dfrac{a}{\sqrt{a^2 + b^2 + c^2}}, \ m = \pm \dfrac{b}{\sqrt{a^2 + b^2 + c^2}}, \ n = \pm \dfrac{c}{\sqrt{a^2 + b^2 + c^2}}$

## Relation Between the Direction Cosines of a Line

If $l$, $m$, $n$ are the direction cosines of a line, then $l^2 + m^2 + n^2 = 1$

## Direction Cosines of a Line Passing Through Two Points

The direction cosines of the line segment joining the points

$A(x_1, y_1, z_1)$ and $B(x_2, y_2, z_2)$ are $\dfrac{x_2 - x_1}{AB}, \dfrac{y_2 - y_1}{AB}, \dfrac{z_2 - z_1}{AB}$

where $AB = \sqrt{(x_2 - x_1)^2 + (y_2 - y_1)^2 + (z_2 - z_1)^2}$

## Equation of a Line

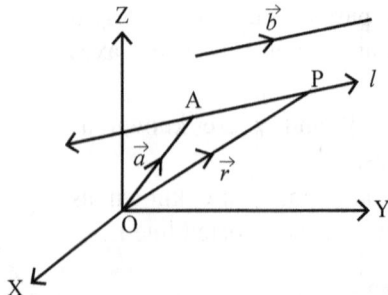

## Vector Equation

The vector equation of the line $l$ which is parallel to vector $b$ and passes through point A is given by

$$\vec{r} = \vec{a} + \lambda \vec{b}$$

where $\vec{r}$ is the position vector of an arbitray point P, $\vec{a}$ is the position vector of the given point A with respect to origin and $\lambda$ is a real number.

## Cartesian Equation

The Cartesian equation of the line that passes through the point $(x_1, y_1, z_1)$ with direction ratios $a, b, c$ is given by

$$\frac{x - x_1}{a} = \frac{y - y_1}{b} = \frac{z - z_1}{c}$$

If $l, m, n$ are the direction cosines, then

$$\frac{x - x_1}{l} = \frac{y - y_1}{m} = \frac{z - z_1}{n}$$

# Equation of a Line Passing Through Two Points
## Vector Equation

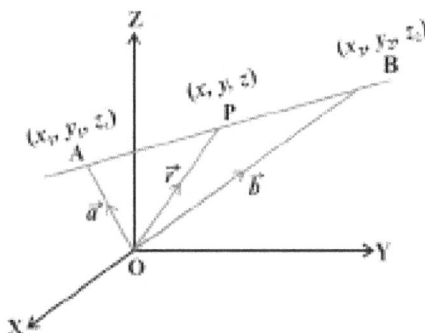

If vector $a$ and vector $b$ are the position vectors of the points A $(x_1, y_1, z_1)$ and B $(x_2, y_2, z_2)$ respectively and vector $r$ be the position vector of an arbitrary point P$(x, y, z)$, then the vector equation is given by

$$\vec{r} = \vec{a} + \lambda (\vec{b} - \vec{a}), \text{ where } \lambda \in R$$

## Cartesian Equation

The cartesian equation of the line joining two points A$(x_1, y_1, z_1)$ and B$(x_2, y_2, z_2)$ is given by

$$\frac{x - x_1}{x_2 - x_1} = \frac{y - y_1}{y_2 - y_1} = \frac{z - z_1}{z_2 - z_1}$$

# Angle Between Two Lines

- The angle $\theta$ between two lines $L_1$ and $L_2$ passing through the origin and with direction ratios $a_1, b_1, c_1$ and $a_2, b_2, c_2$ respectively is given by

$$\cos\theta = \left| \frac{a_1 a_2 + b_1 b_2 + c_1 c_2}{\sqrt{a_1^2 + b_1^2 + c_1^2}\sqrt{a_2^2 + b_2^2 + c_2^2}} \right|$$

- If $l_1, m_1, n_1$ and $l_2, m_2, n_2$ be the direction cosines of two lines $L_1$ and $L_2$ respectively, then the angle $\theta$ between the lines is given by

$$\cos\theta = |l_1 l_2 + m_1 m_2 + n_1 n_2|$$

  (i)  Two lines with direction ratios $a_1, b_1, c_1$ and $a_2, b_2, c_2$ are perpendicular if $\theta = 90°$ or $a_1 a_2 + b_1 b_2 + c_1 c_2 = 0$.
  (ii) Two lines with direction ratios $a_1, b_1, c_1$ and $a_2, b_2, c_2$ are parallel if $\theta = 0°$ or $\dfrac{a_1}{a_2} = \dfrac{b_1}{b_2} = \dfrac{c_1}{c_2}$

# Shortest Distance between Two Lines

In three dimensional coordinate system,

  (i)  the shortest distance between two intersecting lines is zero.
  (ii) the shortest distance between two parallel lines is the perpendicular distance between them.
  (iii) For skew lines the shortest distance is perpendicular to both the lines.

  In space the lines which are neither parallel nor intersecting are known as *skew lines*. They lie in different planes.

# Distance between Two Skew Lines

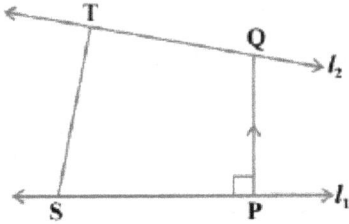

## Vector Form

The shortest distance between two skew lines $l_1$ and $l_2$ with equations $\vec{r} = \vec{a_1} + \lambda \vec{b_1}$ and $\vec{r} = \vec{a_2} + \mu \vec{b_2}$ respectively is given by

$$d = \left| \frac{(\vec{b_1} \times \vec{b_2}) \cdot (\vec{a_2} - \vec{a_1})}{|\vec{b_1} \times \vec{b_2}|} \right|$$

## Cartesian Form

The shortest distance between two skew lines $l_1$ and $l_2$ with equations

$$l_1 : \frac{x - x_1}{a_1} = \frac{y - y_1}{b_1} = \frac{z - z_1}{c_1} \quad \text{and} \quad l_2 : \frac{x - x_2}{a_2} = \frac{y - y_2}{b_2} = \frac{z - z_2}{c_2} \quad \text{is given by}$$

$$\frac{\begin{vmatrix} x_2 - x_1 & y_2 - y_1 & z_2 - z_1 \\ a_1 & b_1 & c_1 \\ a_2 & b_2 & c_2 \end{vmatrix}}{\sqrt{(b_1 c_2 - b_2 c_1)^2 + (c_1 a_2 - c_2 a_1)^2 + (a_1 b_2 - a_2 b_1)^2}}$$

# Distance Between Parallel Lines

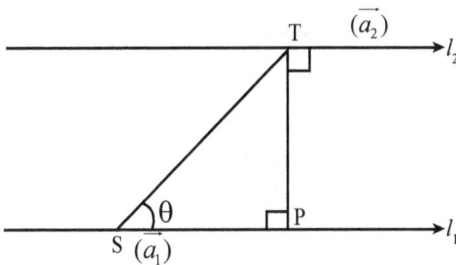

The distance between two parallel lines $l_1$ and $l_2$ with equations $\vec{r} = \vec{a} + \vec{b}$ and $\vec{r} = \vec{a_2} + \mu \vec{b}$ is given by

$$d = |\overrightarrow{PT}| = \frac{|\vec{b} \times (\vec{a_2} - \vec{a_1})|}{|\vec{b}|}$$

A plane is determined uniquely if any one of the following is known:
(i) The equation of a plane in normal form.
(ii) The equation of a plane passes through a given point and perpendicular to a given vector.
(iii) The equation of the plane passes through three non collinear points.

## Equation of a Plane in Normal Form
### Vector Form

If vector $r$ is the position vector of the point $P(x,y,z)$, $d(d \neq 0)$ is the perpendicular distance of the plane from the origin and $\hat{n}$ the unit normal vector along $\overline{ON}$, then the equation of the plane is given by

$$\vec{r} \cdot \hat{n} = d$$

### Cartesian Form
If $l$, $m$, $n$ are the direction cosines and $d(d \neq 0)$ is the perpendicular distance of the plane from the origin, then equation of the plane is given by

$$lx + my + nz = d$$

## Equation of a Plane Passing through a Given Point and Perpendicular to a Given Vector
### Vector Form
If vector $r$ be the position vector of the point $P(x,y,z)$, vector $a$ the position vector of the point Q through which the plane passes and vector N be perpendicular to the plane, then the equation of the plane is given by

$$(\vec{r} - \vec{a}) \cdot \vec{N} = 0$$

## Cartesian Form

If A, B, C are the direction ratios of the vector N and the coordinates of P and Q be $(x,y,z)$ and $(x_1, y_1, z_1)$ respectively, then the equation of the plane is given by

$$A(x - x_1) + B(y - y_1) + C(z - z_1) = 0$$

# Equation of the Plane through Three Non Collinear Points

## Vector Form

If vector $r$ be the position vector of the point $P(x,y,z)$, vector $a$, vector $b$ and vector $c$ be the position vectors of three non collinear points R, S and T respectively, then the equation of the plane is given by

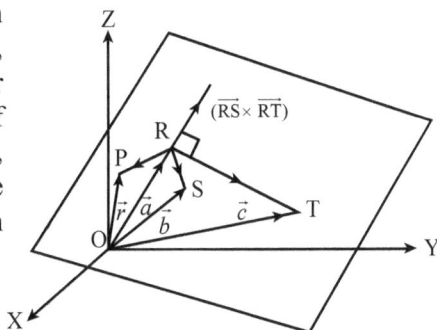

$$(\vec{r} - \vec{a}) \times [(\vec{b} - \vec{a}) \times (\vec{c} - \vec{a})] = 0$$

## Cartesian Form

If vector $r$ be the position vector of the point $P(x, y, z)$, $(x_1, y_1, z_1)$, $(x_2, y_2, z_2)$ and $(x_3, y_3, z_3)$ be the coordinates of the non collinear points R, S and T respectively, then the equation of the plane is given by

$$\begin{vmatrix} x - x_1 & y - y_1 & z - z_1 \\ x_2 - x_1 & y_2 - y_1 & z_2 - z_1 \\ x_3 - x_1 & y_3 - y_1 & z_3 - z_1 \end{vmatrix} = 0$$

# Intercept Form of the Equation of a Plane

The equation of the plane which makes intercepts $a$, $b$, $c$ with $x$, $y$ and $z$ axis respectively is given by $\dfrac{x}{a} + \dfrac{y}{b} + \dfrac{z}{c} = 1$

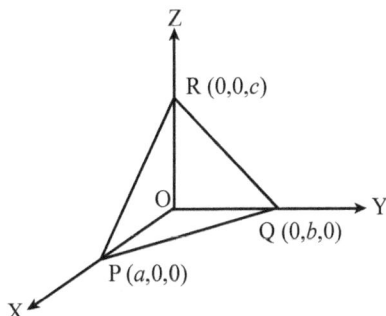

# Plane Passing through the Intersection of Two Given Planes

## Vector Form

If two planes $\pi_1$ and $\pi_2$ have equations $\vec{r} \cdot \hat{n}_1 = d_1$ and $\vec{r} \cdot \hat{n}_2 = d_2$ respectively, then the equation of the plane ($\pi_3$) passing through the intersection of these two planes is given by $\vec{r} \cdot (\vec{n}_1 + \lambda \vec{n}_2) = d_1 + \lambda d_2$ where $\lambda$ is a non zero constant.

## Cartesian Form

The cartesian equation of the plane passing through the intersection of two planes is given by

$$(A_1 x + B_1 y + C_1 z - d_1) + \lambda (A_2 x + B_2 y + C_2 z - d_2) = 0$$

# Coplanarity of Two Lines
## Vector Form

Two lines $\vec{r} = \vec{a}_1 + \lambda \vec{b}_1$ and $\vec{r} = \vec{a}_1 + \mu \vec{b}_1$ are coplanar if and only if $(\vec{a}_2 - \vec{a}_1) \cdot (\vec{b}_1 \times \vec{b}_2) = 0$

## Cartesian Form

If $(x_1, y_1, z_1)$ and $(x_2, y_2, z_2)$ be the coordinates of points A and B respectively and if $a_1, b_1, c_1$ and $a_2, b_2, c_2$ be the direction ratios of vector $b_1$ and vector $b_2$ respectively, then

$$\overline{AB} = (x_2 - x_1)\hat{i} + (y_2 - y_1)\hat{j} + (z_2 - z_1)\hat{k}$$
$$\vec{b}_1 = a_1 \hat{i} + b_1 \hat{j} + c_1 \hat{k} \text{ and } \vec{b}_2 = a_2 \hat{i} + b_2 \hat{j} + c_2 \hat{k}$$

The given lines are coplanar if

$$\begin{vmatrix} x_2 - x_1 & y_2 - y_1 & z_2 - z_1 \\ a_1 & b_1 & c_1 \\ a_2 & b_2 & c_2 \end{vmatrix} = 0$$

# Angle between Two Planes

The angle between two planes is defined as the angle between their normals.

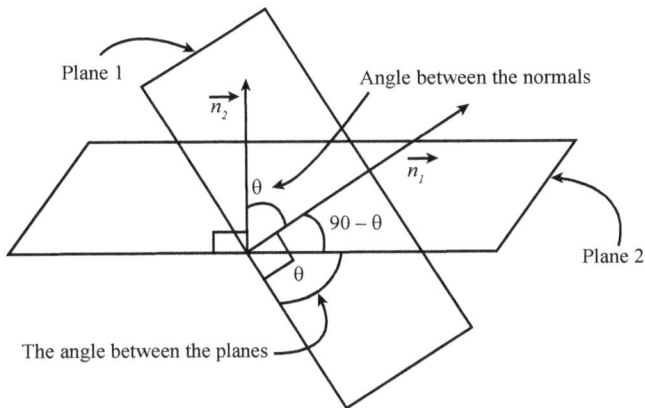

Plane 1

Angle between the normals

$\vec{n}_2$

$\theta$

$\vec{n}_1$

$90 - \theta$

Plane 2

$\theta$

The angle between the planes

## Vector Form

The angle $\theta$ between two planes with normals as vector $n_1$ and vector $n_2$ respectively is given by

$$\cos\theta = \left| \frac{\vec{n}_1 \cdot \vec{n}_2}{|\vec{n}_1| \, |\vec{n}_2|} \right|$$

## Cartesian Form

The angle $\theta$ between two planes,

$A_1x + B_1y + C_1z + D_1 = 0$ and
$A_2x + B_2y + C_2z + D_2 = 0$
is given by

$$\cos\theta = \left| \frac{A_1A_2 + B_1B_2 + C_1C_2}{\sqrt{A_1^2 + B_1^2 + C_1^2} \sqrt{A_2^2 + B_2^2 + C_2^2}} \right|$$

where $A_1$, $B_1$, $C_1$ and $A_2$, $B_2$, $C_2$ are the direction ratios of the normal to the planes respectively.

*Note:*

(i)  If the planes are at right angles, then
$\cos\theta = A_1A_2 + B_1B_2 + C_1C_2 = 0$

(ii) If the planes are parallel, then $\dfrac{A_1}{A_2} = \dfrac{B_1}{B_2} = \dfrac{C_1}{C_2}$

## Distance of a Point from a Plane
### Vector Form

Let P be a point in plane $\pi_2$ with position vector $\vec{a}$

The equation of the unit vector normal to $\pi_2$ is given by $\vec{r} \cdot \hat{n} = \vec{a} \cdot \hat{n}$

The distance PQ from plane $\pi_1$ is given by $|d - \vec{a} \cdot \hat{n}|$

## Cartesian Form

The distance between the point $P(x,y,z)$ and the plane $Ax + By + Cz + D = 0$ is given by

$$\left| \frac{Ax_1 + By_1 + Cz_1 - D}{\sqrt{A^2 + B^2 + C^2}} \right|$$

## Angle between a Line and a Plane

The angle between a line and a plane is the complement of the angle between the line and the normal to the plane.

The angle $\phi$ between the line $\vec{r} = \vec{a} + \lambda\vec{b}$ and the plane $\vec{r} \cdot \vec{n} = d$ is given by

$$\sin(90 - \phi) = \cos\phi = \left| \frac{\vec{b} \cdot \vec{n}}{||\vec{b}| \cdot |\vec{n}||} \right|$$

## ══ SPHERE ══

## Definition

A locus of points in space which are equidistant from a fixed point is called a sphere. It is a three dimensional shape. The shortest distance between any two points on a sphere is known as *geodesic*.

## Standard Equation of a Sphere

If $P(x,y,z)$ is any point on a sphere with centre $C(h,k,j)$ and radius $r$ then the equation of the sphere is given by

$$(x - h)^2 + (y - k)^2 + (z - j)^2 = r^2$$

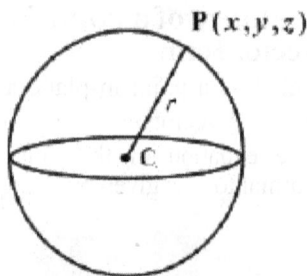

## Equation of a Sphere from the Origin

If $P(x,y,z)$ is any point on a sphere with centre at the origin and radius $r$, then the equation of the sphere is given by $x^2 + y^2 + z^2 = r^2$

## General Equation of a Sphere

The equation of a sphere with centre $(-g,-f, -h)$ and radius $\sqrt{g^2 + f^2 + h^2 - c}$ is given by $x^2 + y^2 + z^2 + 2gx + 2fy + 2hz + c = 0$

where $g, f, h$ and $c$ are contants.

## Equation of a Sphere Passing Through Two Points

If $(x_1, y_1, z_1)$ and $(x_2, y_{2,} z_2)$ are the end points of a diameter, then the equation of the sphere is given by

$$(x - x_1)(x - x_2) + (y - y_1)(y - y_2) + (z - z_1)(z - z_2) = 0$$

## Points on a Sphere

In spherical coordinates, the points on the sphere are given by

$x = r\,sin\phi cos\theta$
$y = r\,sin\phi sin\theta$
$z = r cos\phi$, where $0 \le \theta \le 2\pi, 0 \le \phi \le \pi$

## Great Circle of a Sphere

The section of a sphere that contains the diameter of the sphere is

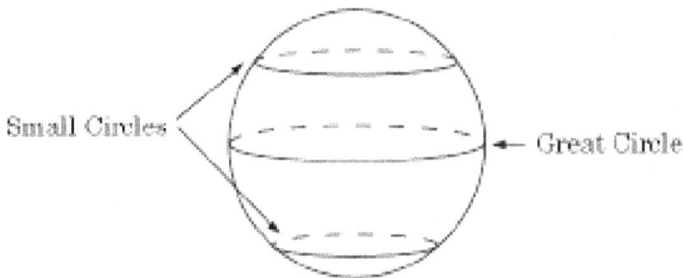

known as the great circle and the section which does not contain the diameter is known as the small circle.

The great circle divides a sphere into two hemispheres.

# 6

## Statistics Formulae

=== **PERMUTATION AND COMBINATION** ===

### Fundamental Principle of Counting (or Multiplication Principle)

If an event can occur in $m$ different ways, following which another event can occur in $n$ different ways, then the total number of occurrence of the events in the given order is $m \times n$.

*For three events*

If an event can occur in $m$ different ways, following which another event can occur in $n$ different ways, following which a third event can occur in $p$ different ways, then the total number of occurrence of the events in the given order is $m \times n \times p$.

*Note:* The fundamental priniciple of counting holds for any finite number of events.

### Factorial $n$

The continuous product of the first '$n$' natural numbers is called factorial $n$ and is deonoted by $n!$ i.e,

$n! = 1 \times 2 \times 3 \times ... \times (n-1) \times n$

$n! = n \times (n-1)!$

$n! = n \times (n-1)(n-2)!$ if $n \geq 2$

$n! = n \times (n-1)(n-2)(n-3)!$ if $n \geq 3$

*Note:*

$0! = 1$ and $1! = 1$

### Permutation

Permutation is an arrangement in a definite order of a number of objects taken some or all at a time.

### Linear Permutation

A permutation is said to be a linear permutation if the objects are arranged in a line. A linear permutation is simply called as a permutation.

## Circular Permutation
A permutation is said to be a circular permutation if the objects are arranged in the form of a circle.

## Formula for Linear Permutation
The number of (linear) permutations that can be formed by taking $r$ things at a time from a set of $n$ distinct things ($r \leq n$) is denoted by $^nP_r$ or $P(n, r)$.

$^nP_r = n(n-1)\,(n-2)\,(n-3)\ldots\ldots (n-r+1)$

where $0 < r \leq n$

$^nP_r = \dfrac{n!}{(n-r)!}, \ 0 \leq r \leq n$

*Note:*

$^nP_n = n!$ and $^nP_0 = 1$

## Number of Permutations Under Certain Conditions
(i) The number of permutations of $n$ objects, where $p$ objects are of the same kind and rest are all different $= \dfrac{n!}{p!}$

(ii) The number of permutations of $n$ objects, where $p_1$ objects are of one kind, $p_2$ are of second kind, ..., $p_k$ are of $k^{th}$ kind and the rest, if any, are of different kind is $\dfrac{n!}{p_1!p_2!\ldots p_k!}$

(iii) Number of permutations of $n$ dissimilar things, taken $r$ at a time, when a particular thing is to be always included in each arrangement, is $r\left(^{n-1}P_{r-1}\right)$

(iv) Number of permutations of $n$ different things, taken $r$ at a time, when a particular thing is never taken in each arrangement is $^{n-1}P_r$

(v) Number of permutations of $n$ different things, taken all at a time, when $m$ specified things always come together is $m!(n-m+1)!$.

(vi) Number of permutations of $n$ different things, taken all at a time, when $m$ specified never come together is $n! - [m!(n-m+1)!]$.

(vii) The number of permutations of $n$ dissimilar things taken $r$ at a time when $k(<r)$ particular things always occur is $[^{n-k}P_{r-k}]\cdot[^rP_k]$.

(viii) The number of permutations of $n$ dissimilar things taken $r$ at a time when $k$ particular things never occur is $^{n-k}P_r$

(ix) The number of permutations of $n$ different objects taken $r$ at a time when repetition is allowed any number of times is $n^r$

(x) The number of permutations of $n$ different things, taken not more than $r$ at a time, when each thing may occur any number of times is

$$n + n^2 + n^3 + \ldots\ldots + n^r = \frac{n(n^r - 1)}{n - 1}$$

(xi) The number of permutations of $n$ different things taken not more than $r$ at a time ${}^nP_1 + {}^nP_2 + {}^nP_3 + \ldots + {}^nP_r$

## Circular Permutation

(i) The number of circular permutations of $n$ dissimilar things taken $r$ at a time when clockwise and anticlockwise orders are taken as different is $\dfrac{{}^nP_r}{r}$.

(ii) The number of circular permutations of $n$ dissimilar things taken all at a time is $(n - 1)!$

(iii) The number of circular permutations of $n$ things taken $r$ at a time in one direction is $\dfrac{{}^nP_r}{2r}$.

(iv) The number of circular permutations of $n$ dissimilar things in clock-wise direction = Number of permutations in anticlock-wise direction = $\dfrac{(n-1)!}{2}$.

## Combination

A selection that can be formed by taking some or all of a finite set of objects is known as combination.

The number of combinations of $n$ dissimilar things taken $r$ at a time is denoted by ${}^nC_r$ or $C(n, r)$ or $\dbinom{n}{r}$.

## Relationship Between Permutation and Combination

${}^nP_r = {}^nC_r \, r!$ where $0 < r \le n$

## Relationship of Combination

(i) ${}^nC_r = \dfrac{n!}{r!(n-r)!}$, $0 < r \le n$

(ii) ${}^nC_r = {}^nC_{r-1}$

(iii) ${}^nC_{n-r} = {}^nC_r$

(iv) ${}^nC_r + {}^nC_{r-1} = {}^{n+1}C_r$

(v) If ${}^nC_r = {}^nC_s \Rightarrow r = s$ or $n = r + s$

(vi) The number of combinations of $n$ things taken $r$ at a time in which

    a) $s$ particular things will always occur is ${}^{n-s}C_{r-s}$

    b) $s$ particular things will never occur is ${}^{n-s}C_r$

c) $s$ particular things always occur and $p$ particular things never occur is $^{n-p-s}C_{r-s}$

(vii) $^{n}C_{0} + ^{n}C_{1} + ^{n}C_{2} + ... + ^{n}C_{n} = 2^{n}$

(viii) $^{n}C_{0} + ^{n}C_{2} + ^{n}C_{4} + ... = ^{n}C_{1} + ^{n}C_{3} + ^{n}C_{5} + ... = 2^{n-1}$

*Note*:

$$^{n}C_{n} = ^{n}C_{0} = 1 \text{ and } ^{n}C_{1} = n$$

## Distribution of Things Into Groups

(i) Number of ways in which $(m + n)$ items can be divided into two unequal groups containing $m$ and $n$ items is $^{m+n}C_{m} = \dfrac{(m+n)!}{m!n!}$.

(ii) The number of ways in which $mn$ different items can be divided equally into $m$ groups, each containing $n$ objects and the order of the groups is not important is $\left[ \dfrac{(mn)!}{(n!)^{m}} \right] \dfrac{1}{m!}$

(iii) The number of ways in which $mn$ different items can be divided equally into $m$ groups, each containing $n$ objects and the order of the groups is important is $\dfrac{(mn)!}{(n!)^{m}}$.

(iv) The number of ways in which $(m + n + p)$ things can be divided into three different groups of $m$, $n$, and $p$ things respectively is $\dfrac{(m+n+p)!}{m!n!p!}$.

═══════════ **PROBABILITY** ═══════════

## Definitions

In Mathematics, Probability is the calculation of uncertainty. It is the measure of how likely an event occurs.

*Experiment* : An action that has various outcomes that occur unpredictably and can be repeated indefinitely under the same conditions. For example, throw of a dice.

*Outcome* : An outcome is the possible result of a single trial of an experiment. For example, tossing of a coin has two possible outcomes – heads or tails.

*Sample Space* : The collection of all possible outcomes of a random experiment is known as sample space. For example, sample space in the throw of a dice = {1, 2, 3, 4, 5, 6}

*Sample Point* : Each element of a sample space is known as a sample point.

*Event* : An event is one or more outcomes of an experiment.

For example, getting an even number in the throw of a dice. An event is a subset of the sample space.

*Experimental or Empirical Probability* : Probabilities based on the results of actual experiments and adequate recordings of the happening of the events are known as experimental or empirical probability.

*Theoretical Probability* or *Classical Probability* : The probability that a certain outcome will occur as determined through reasoning or calculation is known as theoretical probability.

## Probability of an Event

If the experiments have an equally likely outcome, then the classical probability or theoretical probability of an event is given by

$$\text{Probability of an event} = \frac{\text{Number of favourable outcomes}}{\text{Total number of outcomes}}$$

*Important Points on Cards*

- A deck of playing cards consists of 52 cards which are divided into 4 suits - spades (♠), hearts (♥), diamonds (♦) and clubs (♣).
- Two suits are black (clubs and spades) while two are red (hearts and diamonds) in colour.
- Each suit consists of 13 cards namely ace, 2, 3, 4, 5, 6, 7, 8, 9, 10, Jack, Queen and King.
- Kings, queens and jacks are called face cards.

## Types of Event

*Impossible Event :* An empty set is an impossible event.

*Sure Event :* The whole sample space is a sure event.

*Simple Event or Elementary Event* : An event having only one outcome is called an elementary event.

*Compound Event :* If an event has more than one sample point, it is known as a compound event.

## Algebra of Events

*Complimentary Event* : For every event A there corresponds not an event A which is known as complement of A. The complement of A is represented by A' or A$^c$. If S is the sample space, then

A' = S – A = {a : a ∈ S and a ∉ A}

*The Event 'A and B'* : If A and B are two events, then the set A ∩ B denotes the event 'A and B'.

A ∩ B = {$a$ : $a$ ∈ A and $a$ ∈ B}

*The Event 'A or B' :* If A and B are two events, then the set A ∪ B denotes the event 'A or B'.

$A \cup B = \{a : a \in A \text{ or } a \in B\}$

*The Event 'A but not B'* : If A and B are two events, then the set $A \cap B'$ denotes the event 'A but not B'. It is represented by $A - B$.

$A - B = A \cap B'$

## Mutually Exclusive Events

If A and B are two events, then they are called mutually exclusive if they cannot occur simultaneously i.e. if the occurrence of any one of them excludes the occurrence of the other event.

$$A \cap B = \phi, \text{ (A and B are disjoint sets)}$$

## Exhaustive Events

(i) Let S be the sample space and $E_1$, $E_2$, ..., $E_n$ be $n$ events. If $E_1 \cup E_2 \cup E_3 \cup ... \cup E_n = \overset{n}{\underset{i=1}{\cup}} E_i = S$, then $E_1$, $E_2$, ..., $E_n$ are called exhaustive events.

(ii) If $E_i \cap E_j = \phi$ for $i \neq j$ and $\overset{n}{\underset{i=1}{\cup}} E_i = S$, then events $E_1$, $E_2$, ..., $E_n$ are called mutually exclusive and exhaustive events.

## Some Results of Probability

(i) The sum of the probabilities of all possible outcomes of an event of an experiment is 1.

(ii) P(event) + P(not event) = 1

(iii) Probability of an event always lies between 0 and 1 or $0 \leq P(\text{event}) \leq 1$

(vi) Probability of an impossible event is 0, $P(\phi) = 0$

(v) Probability of a sure event is 1.

(vi) If S be the sample space containing elements $a_1$, $a_2$,..., $a_n$, then

  (i) $P(a_1) + P(a_2) + ... + P(a_n) = 1$

  (ii) $0 \leq P(a_i) \leq 1$ for each $a_i \in S$

  (iii) For any event A, $P(A) = \sum P(a_i)$, $a_i \in A$

## Probability Rules

(i) If A and B are any two events of a sample space associated with a random experiment, then the probability the event A or event B occurs is given by: $P(A \cup B) = P(A) + P(B) - P(A \cap B)$

(ii) If two events A and B of a random experiment are mutually exclusive, then

$$P(A \cup B) = P(A) + P(B) \text{ and } P(A \cap B) = 0$$

(iii) If A and B – A are mutually exclusive, then

$$P(A \cup B) = P(A) + P(B - A)$$

(iv) If A ∩ B and B – A are mutually exclusive
$$P(B) = P(A \cap B) + P(B - A)$$
(v) $P(A^C) + P(A) = 1$
or P(not A ) = $P(A^c) = P(A') = 1 - P(A)$
where $P(A^C)$ and P(A') denote the probability of A complement.
(vi) If A, B, C are three events of a sample space associated with a random experiment, then
$$P(A \cup B \cup C) = P(A) + P(B) + P(C) - P(A \cap B) - P(A \cap C)$$
$$- P(B \cap C) + P(A \cap B \cap C)$$

## Conditional Probability

If A and B are two events of a sample space associated with a random experiment, the conditional probability of the event A given that B has occurred is denoted by P(A│B). It is given by

$$P(A \mid B) = \frac{P(A \cap B)}{P(B)} \text{ where } P(B) \neq 0$$

## Properties of Conditional Probability

(i) If A and B are two events of a sample space S associated with a random experiment, then P(S│B) = P(B│B) = 1
(ii) If A and B are any two events of a sample space S associated with a random experiment and C is an event of S such that P(C) ≠ 0, then
$$P((A \cup B) \mid C) = P(A \mid C) + P(B \mid C) - P((A \cap B) \mid C)$$
(iii) If A and B are disjoint events, then
$$P((A \cup B) \mid C) = P(A \mid C) + P(B \mid C) \text{ and } P((A \cap B) \mid C) = 0$$
(iv) If A and B are two events of a sample space S associated with a random experiment and B ≠ φ, then
$$P(A' \mid B) = 1 - P(A \mid B)$$

## Multiplication Theorem of Probability

(i) If A and B are any two events of a sample space associated with a random experiment, then the probability that the event A and event B both occur is given by:
(a) P(A ∩ B) = P(A) P(B|A) where P(A) ≠ 0
(b) P(A ∩ B) = P(B) P(A|B) where P(B) ≠ 0
(ii) If A, B and C are any three events of a sample space associated with a random experiment, then the probability that the event A, event B and event C all occur is given by:
(a) P(A ∩ B ∩ C) = P(A) P(B|A) P(C │ (A ∩ B))
(b) P(A ∩ B ∩ C) = P(A) P(B|A) P(C │ (AB))

## Independent Events

(i) Two events A and B of a sample space associated with a random experiment are known as independent events if the probability of occurrence of one of them is not affected by the occurrence of the other.

(ii) Two events A and B of a sample space associated with a random experiment are independent if $P(A \mid B) = P(A)$ where $P(B) \neq 0$ and $P(B \mid A) = P(B)$ where $P(A) \neq 0$

(iii) Two events A and B of a sample space associated with a random experiment are independent if
$$P(A \cap B) = P(A)P(B)$$

(iv) Three events A, B and C of a sample space associated with a random experiment are said to be mutually independent, if
$$P(A \cap B) = P(A)P(B)$$
$$P(A \cap C) = P(A)P(C)$$
$$P(B \cap C) = P(B)P(C)$$
and $P(A \cap B \cap C) = P(A)P(B)P(C)$

*Note*:

Two events A and B of a sample space associated with a random experiment are said to be dependent if $P(A \cap B) \neq P(A)P(B)$

## Properties of Independent Event

If two events A and B of a sample space associated with a random experiment are independent then,

(i) A and B' are independent

(ii) A' and B are independent

(iii)A' and B' are independent

(iv)P(at least one of A and B) $= 1 - P(A') P(B')$

## Partition of a Sample Space

The events $E_1$, $E_2$, ..., $E_n$ represent a partition of the sample space S if they are pairwise disjoint, exhaustive and have nonzero probabilities.

## Theorem of Total Probability

Let A be any event associated with sample space S and let $\{ E_1, E_2, ..., E_n \}$ be a partition of the sample space such that each of the events $E_1$, $E_2$, ..., $E_n$ has non zero probabilities then

$$P(A) = P(E_1) P(A \mid E_1) + P(E_2) P(A \mid E_2) + ... + P(E_n) P(A \mid E_n)$$

$$= \sum_{j=1}^{n} P(E_j) P(A \mid E_j)$$

## Bayes' Theorem

If A is any event of non zero probability, $E_1$, $E_2$, ..., $E_n$ are $n$ non empty events which constitute a partition of sample space S, i.e. $E_1$, $E_2$, ..., $E_n$ are pairwise disjoint and

$$E_1 \cup E_2 \cup E_3 \cup ... \cup E_n = \bigcup_{i=1}^{n} E_i = S, \text{ then}$$

$$P(E_i|A) = \frac{P(E_i)\, P(A|E_i)}{\sum_{j=1}^{n} P(E_j)\, P(A|E_j)} \quad \text{for any } i = 1, 2, 3, ..., n$$

The events $E_1$, $E_2$, ..., $E_n$ are called *hypotheses*.

The probability $P(E_i)$ is called the *priori probability* of the hypothesis $E_i$

The conditional probability $P(E_i|A)$ is called a *posteriori probability* of the hypothesis $E_i$.

## Random Variable

A random variable is a real valued function whose domain is the sample space of a random experiment.

## Probability Distribution of a Random Variable

The probability distribution of a random variable X is the system of numbers

$$X : x_1 \quad x_2 \quad ... \quad x_n$$
$$P(X) : p_1 \quad p_2 \quad ... \quad p_n$$

where $p_i > 0$, $\sum_{i=1}^{n} p_i = 1$, $i = 1, 2, ..., n$

The real numbers $x_1$, $x_2$, ..., $x_n$ are the possible values of the random variable X and $p_i$ ($i = 1, 2, ..., n$) is the probability of the random variable X taking the value $x_i$ i.e., $P(X = x_i) = p_i$

## Mean of a Random Variable

Let X be a random variable with possible values $x_1$, $x_2$, ..., $x_n$ occurring with probabilities $p_1$, $p_2$, ..., $p_n$, respectively. The mean of X is denoted by $\mu$. The mean of a random variable X is also called the expectation of X. It is represented by E(X) and given by the equation.

$$E(X) = \mu = \sum_{i=1}^{n} x_i p_i = x_1 p_1 + x_2 p_2 + ... + x_n p_n$$

## Variance of a Random Variable

Let X be a random variable with possible values $x_1, x_2, ..., x_n$ occurring with probabilities $p(x_1), p(x_2),..., p(x_n)$ respectively. Let $\mu = E(X)$ be the mean of the random variable, then the variance is given by

$$\sigma_x^2 = \text{Var}(X) = \sum_{i=1}^{n}(x_i - \mu)^2 p(x_i)$$

$$\sigma_x^2 = E(X - \mu)^2$$

Variance is also given by

$\text{Var}(X) = E(X^2) - [E(X)]^2$, where $E(X^2) = \sum_{i=1}^{n} x_i^2 p(x_i)$

## Standard Deviation

The non negative square root of the variance of a random variable is known as the standard deviation of the random variable. It is given by

$$\sigma_x = \sqrt{\text{Var}(X)} = \sqrt{\sum_{i=1}^{n}(x_i - \mu)^2 p(x_i)}$$

## Bernoulli Trials

Trials of a random experiment are called Bernoulli trials, if they satisfy the following conditions:

(i) There should be a finite number of trials.

(ii) The trials should be independent.

(iii) Each trial has exactly two outcomes: success or failure.

(iv) The probability of success remains the same in each trial.

## Binomial Distribution

A binomial distribution with $n$-Bernoulli trials and probability of success in each trial as $p$, is denoted by $B(n, p)$. The probability function $P(X = x)$ or $P(x)$ of the binomial distribution is given by

$$P(x) = {}^nC_x q^{n-x} p^x \qquad x = 0, 1,..., n \quad (q = 1 - p)$$

## ═══════ BINOMIAL THEOREM ═══════

**Binomial Coefficient :** A family of positive integers that occur as coefficients in the binomial theorem is known as binomial coefficient. We use the following formulae of combination to write the binomial coefficient.

$${}^nC_0 = 1 = {}^nC_n \text{ and } {}^nC_r = \frac{n!}{r!(n-r)!}, \ 0 \le r \le n$$

**Pascal's Triangle :** A triangular array of the binomial coefficients is known as Pascal's Triangle.

| Index | Coefficients | | | | | |
|---|---|---|---|---|---|---|
| 0 | | | ${}^0C_0$ (=1) | | | |
| 1 | | ${}^1C_0$ (=1) | | ${}^1C_1$ (=1) | | |
| 2 | | ${}^2C_0$ (=1) | ${}^2C_1$ (=2) | ${}^2C_2$ (=1) | | |
| 3 | ${}^3C_0$ (=1) | ${}^3C_1$ (=3) | ${}^3C_2$ (=3) | ${}^3C_3$ (=1) | | |
| 4 | ${}^4C_0$ (=1) | ${}^4C_1$ (=4) | ${}^4C_2$ (=6) | ${}^4C_3$ (=4) | ${}^4C_4$ (=1) | |
| 5 | ${}^5C_0$ (=1) | ${}^5C_1$ (=5) | ${}^5C_2$ (=10) | ${}^5C_3$ (=10) | ${}^5C_4$ (=5) | ${}^5C_5$ (=1) |

## Binomial Theorem for Any Positive Integer $n$

$$(a + b)^n = {}^nC_0 a^n + {}^nC_1 a^{n-1}b + {}^nC_2 a^{n-2}b^2 + \ldots + {}^nC_{n-1}ab^{n-1} + {}^nC_n b^n$$

where ${}^nC_0$, ${}^nC_1$, ${}^nC_2$, $\ldots$, ${}^nC_n$ are called Binomial coefficients.

The notation $\displaystyle\sum_{k=0}^{n} {}^nC_k\, a^{n-k}b^k$ for

$${}^nC_0 a^n b^0 + {}^nC_1 a^{n-1}b^1 + \ldots + {}^nC_r a^{n-r}b^r + \ldots + {}^nC_n a^{n-n}b^n,$$

where $b^0 = 1 = a^{n-n}$

Thus, the Binomial Theorem can also be written as:

$$(a + b)^n = \sum_{k=0}^{n} {}^nC_k\, a^{n-k}b^k$$

## Properties of Binomial Expansion

(i) The sum of the indices of $a$ and $b$ is $n$ in every term of the expansion.

(ii) There are $(n + 1)$ terms in the expansion of $(a + b)^n$, the first and the last term being $a^n$ and $b^n$ respectively. If ${}^nC_x = {}^nC_y$, then either $x = y$ or $x + y = n$

(iii) The binomial coefficient in the expansion of $(a + b)^n$ which are equidistant from the beginning and the end are equal i.e. ${}^nC_r = {}^nC_{n-r}$.

## Various Binomial Expansions

(i) $(x - y)^n = {}^nC_0 x^n - {}^nC_1 x^{n-1}y + {}^nC_2 x^{n-2} y^2 + \ldots + (-1)^n\, {}^nC_n y^n$

(ii) $(1 + x)^n = {}^nC_0 + {}^nC_1 x + {}^nC_2 x^2 + {}^nC_3 x^3 + \ldots + {}^nC_n x^n$

(iii) $(1 - x)^n = {}^nC_0 - {}^nC_1 x + {}^nC_2 x^2 - \ldots + (-1)^n\, {}^nC_n x^n$

## Sum of Binomial Coefficients

Putting $x = 1$ in the expansion

$(1 + x)^n = {}^nC_0 + {}^nC_1 x + {}^nC_2 x^2 + \ldots + {}^nC_x x^n$, we get,

$$2^n = {}^nC_0 + {}^nC_1 + {}^nC_2 + \ldots + {}^nC_n$$

Maths Formulae For School Students

## General Term and the Middle Term

(i) The $(r + 1)^{th}$ term is known as the general term in the expansion of $(a + b)^n$. It is denoted by $T_{r+1}$

$$T_{r+1} = {}^n C_r a^{n-r} b^r$$

Similarly, the general term in the expansion of $(b + a)^n$ is given as $T_{r+1} = {}^n C_r b^{n-r} a^r$. The terms are considered from the beginning.

(ii) If $n$ is even, the middle term in the expansion of $(a+b)^n$ is $\left(\dfrac{n}{2} + 1\right)^{th}$ term.

(iii) If $n$ is odd, there will be two middle terms in the expansion of $(a + b)^n$ namely $\left(\dfrac{n+1}{2}\right)^{th}$ term and $\left(\dfrac{n+1}{2} + 1\right)^{th}$ term.

(iv) In the expansion of $\left(x + \dfrac{1}{x}\right)^{2n}$, where $x \neq 0$, the middle term is $\left(\dfrac{2n+1+1}{2}\right)^{th}$, i.e., $(n + 1)^{th}$ term, as $2n$ is even.

It is given by ${}^{2n} C_n x^n \left(\dfrac{1}{x}\right)^n = {}^{2n} C_n$ (constant).

This term is called the *term independent* of $x$ or the constant term

═══════════════ **AVERAGE** ═══════════════

## Average of Numbers

(i) In a given data, average is given by
$$\text{Average} = \left(\dfrac{\text{Sum of observations}}{\text{Number of observations}}\right)$$

(ii) If the average of $n_1$ items is $x_1$, the average of $n_2$ items is $x_2$ and the average of $n_3$ items is $x_3$, then
$$\text{Total average} = \dfrac{n_1 x_1 + n_2 x_2 + n_3 x_3}{(n_1 + n_2 + n_3)}$$

(iii) Average of first $n$ natural numbers $= \dfrac{(n+1)}{2}$

(iv) Average of first $n$ odd natural numbers $= n$

(v) Average of first $n$ even natural numbers $= (n + 1)$

(vi) Average of the square of first $n$ natural numbers $= \dfrac{(n+1)(2n+1)}{6}$

(vii) Average of the cube of first $n$ natural numbers $= \dfrac{n(n+1)^2}{4}$

(viii) Average of first $n$ multiples of $x = \dfrac{x(n+1)}{2}$

## Average Age

(i) Let the average of ages of $p$ members of a family be $q$ years. If a new member joins the family, then the new average of ages of all the members becomes $r$ years, then

Age of the new member = $[r + p(r - q)]$ years.

(ii) Let the average of ages of $p$ members of a family be $q$ years. If one of the members leaves the family, then the new average of ages of all the members becomes $r$ years, then

Age of the member leaving the family = $[r + p(q - r)]$ years.

# आत्म–विकास/व्यक्तित्व विकास

Also Available in Hindi

Also Available in Hindi

Also Available in Kannada, Tamil

Also Available in Kannada

Also Available in Kannada

## छात्र विकास

## लोकप्रिय विज्ञान

### प्रश्नोत्तरी की पुस्तकें

### ड्राइंग बुक्स

### चिल्ड्रंस एंसाइक्लोपीडिया

# हिन्दी साहित्य

## संगीत/रहस्य/जादू एवं तथ्य

Also Available in Hindi

# कथा एवं कहानियाँ

NEW All Books Fully Coloured

## बच्चों की कहानियाँ

## माता–पिता विषयक/बाल–विकास

## परिवार एवं कुटुम्ब

## पाक-कला / खान पान

Also available in Hindi

## घर की देखभाल

## सौन्दर्य की देखभाल

## क्लासिक सीरीज

हमारी सभी पुस्तकें www.vspublishers.com पर उपलब्ध हैं

www.ingramcontent.com/pod-product-compliance
Lightning Source LLC
Chambersburg PA
CBHW062218080426
42734CB00010B/1940